GRANDMOTHER EARTH V
1999

Love and Prayers,
Frances and Dean

Other Grandmother Earth Publications:

Ashes to Oaks
Grandmother Earth I
Grandmother Earth II
Grandmother Earth III
Grandmother Earth's Healthy and Wise Cookbook
Kinship
Of Butterflies and Unicorns
Take Time to Laugh: It's the Music of the Soul
The Southern Railway: From Stevenson to Memphis
To Love a Whale
View from a Mississippi River Cotton Sack

From Life Press:

Bloom Where You Are Transplanted
Eve's Fruit
The Mothers of Jesus: From Matthew's Genealogy
Our Golden Thread
Thorns to Velvet

GRANDMOTHER EARTH V
1999

FEATURING
AWARD WINNING
POETRY AND PROSE
FROM THE
1998 GRANDMOTHER EARTH NATIONAL
WRITING CONTEST

Patricia Smith
Frances Brinkley Cowden
Editors

Frances D. Darby
Editorial Assistant

GRANDMOTHER EARTH CREATIONS
Memphis, Tennessee

COVER PHOTOGRAPH BY NEAL HOGENBIRK:

Sam Hunt, a Waretown, New Jersey pinelands resident, playing his banjo

ISBN 1-884289-24-X 9.95

FIRST EDITION: 1999

GRANDMOTHER EARTH CREATIONS
P. O. Box 241986
Memphis, Tennessee 38124

We hopefully will stop to consider
All the blessings we've had since birth;
One of the greatest God has provided
Is our home--Grandmother Earth.

--Embree Bolton

Grandmother Earth Creations
was awarded
the second annual
Business Environmental Award for 1995
by the city of Germantown, Tennessee
Environmental Commission
"...for its pro-active role toward promoting
environmental awareness"
by Sharon Goldsworthy,
Mayor of Germantown.

Grandmother Earth Creations prints all books on recycled paper in accordance with their philosophy of helping to preserve the earth. For the same reason most of the customary blank pages are omitted.

THE JUDGES:

Dr. Tod Marshall
Peggy Vinning
Dr. Rosemary Stephens
Barbara Abbott
Lorraine Smith
Grandmother Earth Staff

CONSOLATION PRIZE

the innocent white envelope belies black disappointments
within; as the winner's names
are called, mine isn't--
the only sure reward for song is the joy of singing

D. Beecher Smith, II

WINNERS' LIST
GRANDMOTHER EARTH V

Poetry:

1st-- "Dubno, Ukraine, October 1942," J.C. Hoffman,
    Fort Smith, Arkansas
2nd-- "Powerless," Timothy D. Welch, Corona Del Mar,
    California
3rd-- "Lines from a Ranger's Notebook," Margaret G.
    Cutchins, Auburn, Alabama
4th-- "Swallows," Elizabeth Howard, Crossville, Tennessee
1st HM-- "Passing the Weapon to the Left: A Husband
    Speaks Out," Cathryn Cofell, Appleton, Wisconsin
2nd HM-- "Ghosts of Fiddle Music," Malra Treece,
    Memphis, Tennessee
3rd HM-- "Morning as Usual," Florence Holmes Ryan,
    Memphis, Tennessee

Haiku:

1st-- "Haiku Trilogy," Floyd S. Knight, Jamestown,
    California
2nd--Charles Johnson, Plainsboro, New Jersey
3rd-- "Dry Leaves," Jennifer A. Jenson, Memphis, Tennessee
4th--Opal Harper Wooldridge, Springfield, Tennessee
5th--Evelyn Foote, Memphis, Tennessee
6th--Delores Hinde, Hot Springs, Arkansas

Short Form:

1st--"To the Dandelion," Betty Gay, Lindsay, Oklahoma
1st HM-- "Give Today Your Best!" Jackie Marie White,
    Blytheville, Arkansas

2nd HM-- "Remembering Her," Russell Strauss, Memphis, Tennessee

3rd HM-- "Forgetful Fogey," Robert S. Shelford, DeLand, Florida

Humor:

1st--"Bear In Mind," Betty Lou Hebert, Coeur d'Alene, Idaho

1st HM-- "Is Anybody Home?" Maureen Cannon, Ridgewood, New Jersey

2nd HM-- "Collision on the Produce Aisle," Russell Strauss, Memphis Tennessee

3rd HM-- "Hello Dolly," Helen Blackshear, Montgomery, Alabama

4th HM-- "Sudden Debt," Floyd S. Night, Jamestown, California

5th HM-- "Olfaction," Lee Ann Russell, Springfield, Missouri

Environmental:

1st-- "In Dubio," Timothy Russell, Toronto Ohio

2nd-- "Winter is my Season," Rosemary Stephens, Memphis

3rd-- "Steel Mill Orinthology," Timothy Russell, Toronto, Ohio

4th-- "Rabbit Hearts," Barbara Browers, Okemos, Michigan

5th-- "Myrtle Warbler," Pat Benjamin, Oak Ridge, Tennessee

Prose:

1st-- "Alice Joy," Florence Bruce, Memphis, Tennessee

2nd-- "Mrs. O'Halloran's Garden," Reese Danley-Kilgo, Huntsville, Alabama

3rd-- "Unforgetable Poetry," Louise Stovall Hayes, Memphis, Tennessee

1st HM-- "Daniel," Martha McNatt, Humboldt, Tennessee
2nd HM-- "The Statue of Liberty," Alice Garrison, West
    Plains, Missouri
3rd HM-- "Jumbo Dreams," Russell H. Strauss, Memphis,
    Tennessee
4th HM-- "Nuts, Anyone?" Blanche A. Bell, Tulsa,
    Oklahoma

Humor:
1st--"The Flight Home," Anne H. Norris, Memphis,
    Tennessee
1st HM-- "Where's Mr. Purdy?" Anne H. Norris, Memphis,
    Tennessee
2nd HM-- "Coming of Age," Ruth C. Wintle, Placentia,
    California
3rd HM-- "Retirement a New Game," Kathy Trower,
    Conway, Arkansas
4th HM-- "Rough Day at Work," Hollis K. Cathey, Ash
    Flat, Arkansas

Editor's Choice:
"Gifts," Reese Danley-Kilgo, Huntsville, Alabama

Environmental:
1st--"Too Late Tomorrow," Hollis K. Cathey, Ash Flat,
    Arkansas
1st HM. "The Last Hook-up," A. H. "Pug" Jones, Hot
    Springs, Arkansas
2nd HM-- "Grandmother Earth and Grandfather Time,"
    Cornelius Hogenbirk, Waretown, New Jersey.

Photograph by Dennis P. Beck

GHOSTS OF FIDDLE MUSIC

Dim ghosts of fiddle music
in the mists of the mountains.
Nothing ever really goes away.

Before the states were states
pioneers brought their fiddles
and old ancestral tunes.

For succeeding generations
they played to ease the pain of living,
to celebrate the joy of life.

At sunset when their work was done,
at weddings, barn dances,
softly, gently, at funerals.

Music over the mountains,
over the valleys,
over cities not yet there.

We hear their haunting voices
singing "Rock of Ages"
from the cabins and the churches.

Do you hear the music in the winds?
In the rustling autumn leaves?
In summer thunder, winter ice?

Melodies blending together
as a canopy above us
to keep us whole and sane.

As we listen
to the distant beat
we step in harmony with those
who walked this way before.

Do you hear your great-grandmother
singing hymns in a rainstorm?

Do you hear a fiddle in the clouds?

Malra Treece

RABBIT HEARTS

I will not walk this trail again

Bulldozers wait in that field of asters
trees already captives of lizard-tongue
yellow plastic

Where woodpeckers once shattered air
chain saws buzz like mechanized bees

and rabbit hearts freeze
at shadows that stun the sun

Barbara Brent Brower

DUBNO, UKRAINE, OCTOBER 1942

Before fire could touch stone hearths
and warm away the night, we were marched,
driven by leering soldiers who regarded
with levity my uncloaked breasts and blushing
thighs until one old woman gave me
a thin cotton coat marked by the Star of David,
then shivered her nakedness into strength.
As we counted off
                SS officers touched
the prettiest and motioned them out,
so I became shameless when they passed,
throwing my loaned coat to the ground,
thrusting my breasts,
and punishing a smile on my lips.
My family embraced good-bys
without weeping. They would not look
toward me, but fell
to the crack of rifles like flowers
hammered onto a steel tray.

Now I wish the ragged coat with the hated
yellow patch back on the woman
who gave it, that she might have gone warmly
into the pit, and I could forget her
that I might rest.
That I might sleep at night.

J.C. Hoffman

POWERLESS

Last night the power went out and clocks died in a blinking
   fit,
convulsing without end, while the milk turned sour and all
   the ice

melted into a collective mess born out of the part of itself
it so desperately wants to become, where it should feel
   most safe

and real, as a puddle on the floor. And the moths in their
   nightly ritual
went their separate ways into those fearful shadows, a step
   beyond

the porch now smothered in thick nothingness. The TV
found itself speechless, and of course remembered little of
   the incident

like the coffee machine and the bread maker full of yeast
   and bubbles,
mixing a drunken concoction like a baker coming home late
   from the pub.

My alarm shimmered all too innocently of abilities beyond
   its control
and the ansaphone caught amnesia in total shock. Did she
   call or didn't

she? I'll never know and he'll never say. So I light a candle,
not only for light but for darkness, and for the traveling
   cloud of muggers

that descend like locusts on city blocks, indiscriminate and
    thirsty
for whirring electrons. And the only thing they leave behind
    to let us

know of their presence is the complaints of our things, like
    their dignities
were stolen in a flash of night, hit over the head with a club
    in a dark

alley, tied to walls and strung together like gagged hostages,
    murmuring
something religious, something pure as lightning.

Timothy D. Welch

HAIKU

The starting gates clanged
Like arrows released from bow
Beating hooves thundered

Horses working out
Sun rising like golden disk
Dawn at the backstretch

Anne Marie Dyer

5

LINES FROM A RANGER'S NOTEBOOK

The young bear laps moonsilver
from the river,
takes a trout with ease.
He rises, dripping beads of light,
and leans toward reeds
and motherscent.

Boulders, stark under moonsnow,
are bear-shaped statuary
in my wilderness garden,
Rings of white crowfoot
flower in the path I must take
to paperwork,
tomorrow's unruly tourists.

Resolve to preserve this fragile scene
rises in me
fiercely
like the young bear's hunger.
Together we eye a moonfish
in the river's sheen.

I recall the snowscape,
clean,
suspended
in a clear, glass globe
Uncle Henry brought me from Buffalo
when I was nine,
and find bear, river, boulders, moon

becoming a song that nourishes,
that celebrates.

Margaret G. Cutchins

HAIKU TRILOGY

TO DAWN--

Following the rain,
Sunlit, from a tilted leaf
Molten silver drops.

-- TO NOON

Intimately close,
Bees gossip and drone secrets
To a sleeping cat.

-- TO DUSK

Soft, at close of day,
From dust-filled, long-shadowed lanes
Homebound cowbells ring.

Floyd S. Knight

PASSING THE WEAPON TO THE LEFT: A HUSBAND SPEAKS OUT

In ancient Japan, a man
could divorce his wife
if he discovered she was left-handed.
I wonder if this is cause enough
to be rid of my wife in Wisconsin,
pause at the mirror to confirm
my German heritage. No luck.
It's all in her hands. Purely Oedipal.
Takes after her father. Sucked her thumb
until almost thirteen, even now
when nightmares toss her like a salad.
Hands that never sleep. Two-by-four
tough, they gripe all day all week
at boardroom tables and men's battered egos.
Signal flags at a cocktail party.
Flail about poetry early when
the house tastes of night and hazelnut coffee.
Burrowing out of our dull marriage.
I prefer dull, to plod through life
one project ticked off a list,
one intention at a time,
hand over hand. She, on the other hand--
forgive the cliché--is perpetual
motion: fingers to hair to mouth to itch to
flick to fidget to whisper to stroke.
Oh yes, to stroke.
I've been riding this relationship like a city bus.
Wide corners, no place to sit, strange faces
on and off, on and off, no exact change--
her deep voice on the intercom:
Pull the cord if you want me to stop.
Easter weekend, we made plaster statues

8

of our hands. All ten of my fingers broke off
in the wax mold. She fixed me up with glue
and spackle, put my thumb on backwards.
It's an inside joke, the way she gets me
to point in opposite directions. We
look eye to eye at her perfectly cast left hand
and all its infinite details and for just one moment
she is still. She sees herself as I see her.
Two left hands, a sure sign of Satan. Insanity.
Witchcraft and other clumsy attempts at my heart.

Cathryn Cofell

HAIKU

Holly berries dot
the edge of winter's tailgate...
jonquils blossom gold.

Florine Petkoff Walters

THE WELLS OF ISAAC

"Isaac dug anew the water wells which had been dug in the
days of his father, Abraham . . ."   Genesis 26:18

When Isaac rested at Rehoboth and at Beer-sheba,
He prayed for the rebirth of water amidst jagged
rocks
That loomed brown and mottled
Like the sides of a camel-hair tent.
Then he would choose one pointed flint and dig
Until life gushed like heart-blood from the earth.
Soon curls of grass would form around the rim
Like fringes on a priestly robe.
Earthworms would drill their tunnels through the soil.
Then hoopoes would strut like gaudy princes
Into a courtyard of tender reeds,
And lilies would primp above the mirrored pool.
The hyrax would hide in its clandestine burrows,
And the scarlet ibis would come to wade.
In time, the fragrant fig tree and the sheltering willow
Would block the rays of the raging sun.
Laden with labdanum and gold,
Caravans would stop to drink,
And sandaled sages fanned by the flapping palms
Would unroll their sacred scrolls
And praise the God of fiery father Abraham
And of shrewd son Jacob
And of Isaac, the humble patriarch and preserver,
Who paused to dig wells in the wilderness.

Russell Strauss

SWALLOWS

Mudpie holes line the bank
of the chattering brook;
silver minnows dart

about to float darkly
in the shadows of stones,
smooth as toasted loaves

from a primitive oven.
Beyond the bridge
which a spring deluge

broke into fragments
like sacramental bread,
scores of swallows

line the rusty fence,
air tense, fluttery,
fledglings chattering.

By twos and threes, they
swoop over the golden
wheat, swirl, and return--

back and forth, winnowing
the field for silver insects,
harvesting their staff of life.

Elizabeth Howard

From: *Twilight Ending,* 4:2, May 98

WHERE IS THE PEACEABLE KINGDOM

Dressed in black, her graying hair
in a Gibson Girl bun,
she looked like someone's grandmother.
But she'd drawn the attention of fellow travelers
on the Frisco Pullman
by her repeated and loud counting
on the fingers of one hand:
"One, two, three, four, five."
When they began to laugh,
the man beside her spoke,
"Please stop staring at my wife.
I'm taking her to the asylum;
she's lost five sons in the war,
all killed in action."

Her pride shining though tears
she'd watched them leave, one by one,
marching to the rhythm of John Philip Sousa;
flags flying; townsfolk cheering.
This was "a war to end all wars."

The letters she'd received
told only of trivia.
No mention of the crack of gunfire;
the booming of explosives;
No mention of muddy trenches,
hunger, fatigue, fear,
as much of killing as of dying.

One, two, three, four, five sons;
five stars in the window;

12

five telegrams;
five neatly-folded flags.

Nellie Jones

HAIKU

Soft creek music blends
in songs of woodland thrushes
and whispering pines.

Opal Harper Wooldridge

TO THE DANDELION

Oh, hardy flower, disdained as weed,
Despised for heads of feathery seed,
Your unsung virtues rate a ballad,
Choice roots for wine, crisp leaves for salad.

Betty Gay

BE STILL AND KNOW

Our jet exhausted sky is still draped with God's rainbow
Our million dollar orchards are still rustled by His breeze.
Our livelihood and sustenance depend upon His elements.
Earth's sophisticated tapestry is threaded with His trees.

Our rivers, lakes, and playgrounds are filled by His
        outpouring.
Our bronze and beautiful bodies turn gold beneath His rays.
Our fiber optic highways, suspended through His space.
Communicate the rise of man while these animals give him
        praise.

Victoria Hodge

HAIKU

In the shade beneath
oak trees poets gather words
that fall like acorns.

Charles H. Johnson

CAPTURED

We do not capture time...
it captures us on its winding spool,
that inexorable spindle
turning each day away--
turning each passing season,
each passing year;
while our radiant hours of youth
spin off the spool and fall
in many-colored ribbons--
some pale, some bright--
to drift in long dissolving tides
in a lovely drift
to lift and fall
in cresting waves
to a lost beach of tide-strewn shells
shifting in the moonlight
in white ever-flux.

Winifred Hamrick Farrar

DRY LEAVES

Whistling through dry leaves,
The fall wind spreads the fragrance
Of the dying year.

Jennifer A. Jenson

THE BIG PICTURE

Staring out into blackboard blankness,
ten floors above the ninety degree blast
Of a manhole furnace, penned hair blown
Out of place by a hot, eastern gust,

Behind portable wire-rimmed windows, the security
of vision returns through the aid of ancient
street lamps below. she braves the heights
for a roof-top view of a vacant coffeehouse,
a neighboring fruit market, a lipstick-message-marked
butcher's window with neon gang graffiti.

She stumbles up to the bigger view,
buildings - nice, parallel, and perpendicular, not pretty,
practical like a snowcone for the sweltering sweat-on-the-
          doorstep summer,
just rows of ladder-clad boxes, hole-poked for life.

It's all lonely, fading with the night
when only the noise remains, cars, trucks, planes -
a soundtrack to be sampled.
She sits alone and apart.
She is the culture queen occupied with her space
from the top of a building slightly taller than the rest.

Michael Kass

THE SCATTERING

As the fog crawls across the pond,
they stand waiting
for the boat.
The girl clutches a black box
filled with her mother's ashes.
After climbing aboard
the two brothers and their sister
take turns
sending off their mother.
Quickly the ashes disappear
deep into the cool water
as if burdened, like their mother's life.

Margot Marler

If you were very ill
and dying,
how different your days
would be.
And suppose
you had no God
or heaven,
where to
and how
would you sail away?

Margot Marler

MY FACE

Reflected in the Mirrors of My Rooms

Roses flame the cheeks,
Eyes are silk enamel blue,
Smiles flow from every mirror
in our house; Papa's beveled one
above the hearth, Grandma's
gilded one in entry hall, Mama's
compact in my beaded purse,
one that went to parties, church,
and to the end of things.

Roses fade, but captive wisdom
spirits back the whisper part
of sighted truth; lover lost,
mishap birth, symphonies,
ocean sounds. A capsized life,
retrieved, lost not to sea,
but harbored in my flesh,
ghost written on my mirrored face.

Judith Bader Jones

MAGNOLIA LEGACIES

I lie midnight tranquil
while the groin of my mind
diffuses time to a Delta bayou

where innocuous Tom Sawyer siblings
break the barrier of wilderness
into radiant screams...

flashing naked thighs
across murky, turtle water
in an encyclopedia of dives and splashes
as the salient sun burns dappled mosaics
on the bayou jungle
and the fervid afternoon wears on...
opening its cotton-boll petals at last
(like July four o'clocks)
to twilight and the sorrowing songs
of departing field hands
melting like an African drum-beat
into emerald air,
while the venerable land
keeps its burden of bones
of Choctaw artifacts, secure
and bronzed Olympians traipse home
heavy with magnolia legacies...
with secrets of words not yet spoken.

Frieda Beasley Dorris

SILENT SUPPER

Supper is always the same.
Six plates make white circles
on oil-cloth once sunshine yellow.
Father sits at the head of the table.
Mother fidgets at the opposite end.
Four children sit on benches
like Sunday parishioners in their pews
singing a difficult song.
My oldest sister twists her braids.
A frown purses her lips.
My youngest sister unfolds her napkin,
runs a finger across a pointed pleat.
She folds it back into a square.
My brother runs his fingers around his water glass.
He brings them away, wet.
I stare at the white circles on the table.
My circle has a chip.

Metal forks scrape the glass plates.
Spoons tap on wooden bowls.
Utensils "clunk" and "clink"
like a chorus out of key.
Father looks stern.
There is no other expression on his sunburned face.
His thoughts seem vacant in this room,
lost to a field of amber wheat
or cattle stanchions in the barn.
Mother chews as if by rote.
Her hands move from plate to mouth,
rough, and red, and chapped.
A wistful look fills her eyes,
as if she longs to be somewhere
where it is cool, and soft, and solitary blue.

Seldom do we talk.
Words are frozen like squares
in ice-cube trays, difficult to slide out,
or they evaporate as soon as they are free.
Above my head, a fly buzzes.
He is trying to get out.
Like me, he doesn't know how.

Arla M. Clemons

GIFTS

In Memory of Daniel A. Hannah
Oct. 25, 1981--Dec. 5, 1996

Earth and sky in rainbow hues
With Nature's songs of praise
And fragrance pure as morning's dew
He freely gives each day--
He who lifts our blazing sun
Across snow capped pinnacles
And moves the moon from east to west
Is the same great God
Who gives taste to wild strawberries
And oh, to me he gives the feel
Of April's balmy breeze
With the nuzzle of my infant
Grandson on my cheek...

Burnette B. Benedict

MOMENTS AGO

I don't care that once moist
the clay's now been set. really, I don't.
this scar is the least of my worries.   you see, Doctor,
for six months now
I've been trying to keep at arms length...there

when you have me raise
then place the palm of my hand on top of my head
press into my lymph nodes...there. so I really don't care

that moments ago you weren't too happy
when you lifted my johnny
saw the scar across my breast
as way too red, because, Doctor,

I can hear the winter's cold rain beating
against this thick, glass plated window and I'm afraid...and
I only know

I've been trying not to find
another lump, cyst, or thickening. and, Doctor,

I'm not smiling because you've reassured me,
but for the reason that, somehow,
you know how to speak to me
(in a metaphor? are you a poet?):

"every time you go out in your car, you must know
you could be in an accident
but that doesn't keep you from driving."

I know. but, Doctor, right now
I 'm crossing this parking lot, going home, already twilight

and remembering
when as a child

evenings were so slow to fall.

Barbara A. Rouillard

WORD DREAMS

Words swell up within
hauntingly hounding
my sleep
they speak to me
in complete paragraphs
the story presents itself
I wake
it's 2:00 a.m.
I must go to sleep again.
Morning shakes me
from deep slumber
I rise
pen reaches paper
sentence begun
but the story has run
away.

Debra Parmley

From: *Rainbows End*

BUT FOR GRACE

I see her every day

pushing her loaded cart, jealously
guarding a broken picture frame, some faded
plastic flowers, a shawl, a candy box;

the jumbled cast-off pieces

of ordinary lives, collected carefully,
and made her own. I've heard her scream
obscenities at those who come too near.

I know that scream.

Those who have faced the frailities
of fear feel every nuance of its voice.
The world is a scary place, you know,

when rain falls cold,

when dreams are gone. We all live on
the jagged edge of city-splintered night.
We all cling to objects.

Linus has his blanket.

I have mine. I hope that hers is warm,
that her hidden hoard of small change
buys a bottle and a book.

And as each midnight mist

drifts down on cold concrete,

warm wine, I hope that painted petals,
in a streetlight's molten glow,

begin to tremble,

then to open wide. If only for
a moment, if only in a dream, I hope
one plastic rose will bloom for her.

Jeanne Heath Heritage

WHERE HAVE THE CHILDREN GONE

(Of Friends and Relatives, Beware)

The three of them went out to play.
I did not say,
"Be careful now."
They all knew how
to look both ways to cross a street
and would not greet
an unknown man;
instead they ran.
But Uncle Joe said, "Climb right in,
we'll take a spin.
The lake is deep
for final sleep.

Ida Crane Walker

25

MAMA'S SHOES

I

Wire rim bifocals stare
from the piano top,
watching mute ivories grooved
by countless caresses.
Possessions, prized by Mama,
sit in disarray. A sweater snag,
calling for attention, goes unmended.
My heart lies unstirred, deadened,
numb. A haze of disbelief
dims my vision. Stumbling, I grasp
the door frame. Adrenalin quickens,
at my feet, I discover
Mama's empty shoes.

II

Good-bye, Mama. One year
late. A year since morphine
quelled your pain, stole
our final time together.
A year of denial, looking
past your clothes, your shoes,
your silent piano. Today,
I packed boxes, left them
at the Mission, drove home,
and played your favorite hymns
with one finger.

III

Only memories remain
of the shoes I left at the Mission
today. I pray they protect a bag lady's
feet from the cold. Barely worn,
they weren't old. Chair-bound,
Mama wore them on church-day
at the Home. A crooked grin stroke-pasted
on her face, she'd say, "I never was hard
on shoes--like you." Then as old voices
quavered the final hymn to an uncertain
end, she'd wheel to her room, pack them
into their box, and ask,
"Do I know you?"

Ann Hoffman

CONFINED

Just guilty of age
Now imprisoned and confined
Frail bone body cage

Delores Hinde

NIGHTTIME

Little girls in sundresses
And little boys in overalls
Running barefoot through monkey-grass
On the hottest night they've ever seen
Chasing fireflies with jelly jars
While a too-old hound rests his good eye
On a porch that needs to be painted
Never notice the contrast
Of clouds against the midnight sky.
The ice-cream man, snoring in his bed,
Can taste the air
It's so thick
And can hear the melancholy mantra
Of chimes singing
With the gentle winds
And the cries of thirsty crickets and the toads
Playing a euphonic backup.
A bird roosted on a wooden mailbox
That has been replaced twice
Every year since they moved into that house
Smells an apple festering on top of the soil
And two trout pinned to a clothesline.

Carly Kiel

PIE IN THE SKY

Whipped
Into a
Frothy, rich meringue,
Egg-white-clouds
Were tapped
Upon the rim
And
Spooned haphazardly
Over a
Blue custard
On a crust
Of flaky brown.

Lois Batchelor Howard

HATE

Lying silently in wait,
Black emptiness the only trait
For this curious, vicious snake
That slowly squeezes until you ache.

Teeth are biting, gnashing
Dizziness, the lights flashing
Ever slowly it eats away
While the heart begins decay.

Rebecca Earle

IN DUBIO

Smoke plumes coil in the valley
like cavalry dust, and irises
so purple they must ache, bloom
in front of the white block wall,
but rescue is still improbable here
where the moon is as likely
to pass behind heated vapors
rising from a boiler house stack,
as if it were a lemon slice
sinking in some summer drink,
as it is to catch a locust branch,
delicate and vaguely Oriental,
lying across it like scrimshaw,
the same hour, the same night,
where cardinals nest in the wisteria,
Baltimore orioles in the sycamore,
and sparrows in the air conditioner,
where fresh asparagus is exotic,
and men tend machinery all night
as if it were troubled livestock.

Timothy Russell

THE SADDEST WORDS

Remember when we
could see stars in the heavens
and hear songs of birds.

Marjorie Millison

NOTE: I was in Tokyo in 1972. Our Japanese guide
(approximately 30 years of age) told us, "When I was a boy
I remember seeing stars in the sky, there were song birds
and garden flowers." We saw no stars, no song birds, no
garden flowers. We were fortunate to have gotten a glimpse
of Mt. Fuji during our four day stay. I've never forgotten.

HAIKU

A mist-sheathed shoreline
Eroding in wild sea tears
That no sun consoles.

Ruth Peal Harrell

Photograph by Michael Lucas

SNOW CRYSTALS

Winter diamonds
lightly strewn
on a ribbon of
asphalt

J. Harding

REMEMBERING HER

Her life, elusive firefly,
Flickered in the night.
You could not cup your hand
To trap its fleeting light.

Russell Strauss

HAIKU

Independence Day
The colors of freedom fly
Cardinal, dove, bluejay

Anne Marie Dyer

Laughing Seagulls - *Larus atricilla*

Photograph by Neal Hogenbirk

FLIGHT

I want to go lightly
when I leave,
like the fledgling bird
who quits the nest
and falls into the air,
gives himself wholly
to that falling
and finds his wings.
I want to remember
how to fly.

Therese Arceneaux

Morning. White egrets
      soar in formation, early
      sunlight on their wings.

Therese Arceneaux

BY WATER'S EDGE

The majestic, white crane
stands firmly on one leg,
motionless in the breeze.
He looks into the pool
as his reflection sways.
As his reflection sways
gently within the blue,
a pebble disturbs it,
causing it to shatter
like shards of broken glass.

Diane M. Clark

Inspired by a saying of
Kawada Jun
The Little Zen Calendar
July 7, 1997

HAIKU

shimmer on the sidewalk
old tattered woman kneels
to gather her coins

Leonardo Alishan

ALLEY CAT

In floppy hat with plastic flowers pinned
So long ago the pinks have weathered gray,
A cagey lady sneakers into wind
That blows the sour breath of fruit decay.
Behind a shopping cart with wobbly wheels,
She rolls her world along a cluttered street,
And home is where a shelter offers meals
Or garbage cans are props for swollen feet.
The ghetto nights have beaten laughter off
Her crinkled face of coffee-colored stain,
And when her body quakes in spasm-cough,
A dirty raglet catches liquid pain,
    But still she prowls as huntress in the wild,
    An alley cat with eyes of wounded child.

Kitty Yeager

HAIKU

stitched with skillful care
and women's tireless patience
old quilts speak of love

Evelyn Foote

BISON

A glide of grassland.
They stand like moonmarks
Stamped upon the prairie
Where no human is supposed
To travel.
For an instant, the buffalo
Are blades of grass and
Something has spoken
To their roots and areoles.
Buffalo again, the signal
Starts in an eye corner,
Spreads through them
In flashes of lightning.

They are galloping now,
Trying to outrun arrows,
Outfly bullets, knowing better,
the sound of their dead
Thudding in their ears.
They are galloping now,
Their hooves splashing the light,
And their flesh is caught
on thorns of wind
As they and the grass race.
Speed envelops them.
They disappear, brown
Into brown mountains,
Horns filling with run-sound,
Their firebones melting
In the last strokes of sun.

June Owens

FORGETFUL FOGEY

a Clerihew

Methusaleh was quite a guy
Nine hundred years and still quite spry
He chased the girls, then made them cry
For he could not remember why.

Robert S. Shelford

AUTUMN WINDS

Autumn winds
pulling & tugging,
waiting for me...
to leave my home,
find my destiny.
To float on air,
to see and be free,
but only for a moment--
and then I must be
just another leaf
under this old oak tree.

Tracy Patterson

ONE WINTER NIGHT

Night closes like a black silk purse
clasped by the moon
bejeweled with stars.
A wind rises
stirring bare branches
moving across the dimming moon.

Without so much as a whisper,
the storm covers the brick
along the walkway
blowing clear
cold legends upon the outside of the
windowpanes.

Edith Guy

GIVE TODAY YOUR BEST!

Each day is a challenge; no two are the same.
You win some and lose some in life's daily game.
So whatever your purpose, whatever your quest,
Since tomorrow's uncertain, give today your best!

Jackie Marie White

YOU CAN'T SLEEP WITH POETRY

The year my husband died
and people said consolingly,
"It's good you have your poetry,"
I yearned to scream,
        "But you can't walk or talk
                or sleep with poetry!"

The un-bereaved don't see
        the poverty of life alone.
Alone, I grasp for bits of family and friends.
A phone to ring. Letters to read. A touch.
        How will my end come?
        Who will care if I hurt?

Unneeded - but to care for my own needs,
I feed on foods rejected by nutrition books
and sleep when I'm too tired to care
        this bed has room to spare.
My face relearned a smile, and laughter
        lilts to tilt the scale away from pity.

I won't chain children to my grief. Let them
believe that clubs, poetry and their
                brief visits satisfy
                this wedding remnant.
They must not feel the vacuum
in this house when they come home.

Alone, I seek strength to live alone,
        weep alone

sleep alone
in this strange stanza of my life
while I instruct my missing sonnet heart
to write free verse.

Verna Lee Hinegardner

ADOLESENCE

the loneliness--
the grey seemingly endless
sunless days
then the light
rush to the warmth
stunning
abandonment
rising temperatures
unexplained
inner combustion

Frank Govan

Heath Aster - *Aster pilosus*

Photograph by Neal Hogenbirk

43

STILL WATERS

The waterfall, roaring over the dam,
mirrors the magenta sunset, the mottled
sycamores. Golden ragwort lines
the banks, a heron hunts among velvet
cattails in a slough, a kingfisher
dives into the blue hole by the swinging
bridge. In the still waters beyond, a boy
fishes, tossing out, drawing in; the lure
glimmers in the light like a dragonfly's
wing. Another boy collects driftwood,
lays it on the campfire ashes, blows
the smoldering logs, coughing when the smoke
billows in his face. He fetches the speckled
trout idling on the string in the icy
water, cleans them on a boulder, drops them
in the sizzling skillet. The smell of frying
fish mingles with the scent of hickory
smoke. As the boys wait, one whistles
a tuneless strain, the other pokes stubborn
firewood. Evening shadows lengthen, dapple
the water with silhouettes of mutant phantoms;
a chill pervades the air, a screech owl whimpers.
Stomachs stuffed, the boys draw closer
to the fire, away from the dark forest
and secret monsters which lie in still waters.

Elizabeth Howard

Published in *Potpourri: A Magazine of the Literary Arts*,
9:4, 97

HARLEQUINS

(for yvette)

when i was fifteen
i would save up 2 dollars 50 cents
for a stroll through b. dalton's
to buy
passion flower in rome
december love in may
escape to a paris romance
incognito
(did you do this too?)
always incognito
dark handsome white man
waiting
in the wings
and somehow between books
i'd overlook
the deceptions
and inconsistencies between
the pages and my blackness
the last two chapters
and my ambi skin tone skin
and for half a second
book freshly closed
(did you do this too?)
words lingering still
i would move beyond
brown body/
full lips/
smile into a looking glass
pinch life into pale cheeks
and comb
my long

blond hair
while dying

Lurlynn Franklin

TULIPS THROUGH THE SNOW

Into our daily lives
troubles come and troubles go.
Some are like winter days
with winds cold with snow.

We feel so overwhelmed
that we give in to despair.
Nothing looks alive
in the cold winter air.

With each passing day,
this I surely know,
Our spirits survive adversity.
Our souls continue to grow.

We wait and gather our strength,
then let our determination show.
We overcome the winter of despair
like tulips through the snow.

Allan Gilbreath

IS ANYBODY HOME?

I used to grow old
When they put me on 'hold,'
And I waited in silence, a martyr,
But the fashion today
Is to make *music* play,
And to soothe with a gentle sonata,
Or a silvery flute,
Or the song of a lute
Guaranteed to.prevent me from groaning
As I glance at the clock.
Listen, don't give me Bach,
Give me simply the person I'm PHONING?

Maureen Cannon

HAIKU

A lone hawk circles;
winter approaches like death --
silent on dark wings.

Charles H. Johnson

SEASONED OUT

                I
longed for
an
early summer to release
tree-barked butterflies ...
The sun
answered like a huge
once over easy fried
egg in a blue-skillet
sky...
The sweat bees knew where to find me ...
and now...
I long for an early
winter and
blue rain to
sing the
butterflies
back
to sleep.

Patty Hoye Ashworth

WINTER IS MY SEASON

Winter is my season: cold, clear,
calm -- a time to grow old peacefully,
shawl-wrapped,
not for eruption joys, not for painful birth.
Winter wears sapphires, soft slippers
and a cape fur-lined.
She sits quietly in the dark whiteness.
In Winter I can see the dead squirrels' nests up high
through bare branches where birds
now flown once sang on key.
And at night the whole near-world is star-touched
as bright snow rims the smooth
uninterrupted earth.

Rosemary Stephens

From: *Old Hickory Review*

HAIKU

Snow falling gently
Silently covering ground
Turns night into day.

Eleanor Moore

IN THE CORE OF THE SUN

In the core of the sun
There is a sparrow's egg
Lying with security
    absorbing the boiling of the sun
    weaving it into mornings

Kareem Al-Darahi

A CHILD LOOKING
FOR A CONTINUAL FRIEND

The children came of age
While the dwarf was still a child
So he associated with new children
But they were also struck
    with adulthood

Kareem Al-Darahi

THE ANCIENT MIDWIVES

salted and blessed the newborns.

I used to wonder at that
thinking of how salt corrodes
how life has too much salt to it
in circles on a tired man's shirt.
A face alone at night.

Salt.

But waking this day in a rush of predawn wind
smart as a callused slap
I see the salty benediction:
salt cleans
heals
preserves.

The ancient midwives knew
what a grand good starter
salt can be.

                    Dodie Messer Meeks

BEAR IN MIND

The threshing crew had eaten,
The dishes put away.
My aunt and mother's chores were done,
Until another day,
The moon outside was brilliant.
It beckoned them out there.
My uncle hollered at them,
"Be careful of the bear."
"What bear is that?" my aunt replied.
She gave my mom a wink,
"The bear I saw last evening,
He's after pigs, I think.
His footprints are gigantic
And he trampled down some grain.
So keep your eyes wide open,
If you wander down the lane."
The women closed the door and laughed.
They thought he was a tease.
The smell of smoke and wheat was borne
Upon the autumn breeze,
The walk was long and lovely
And as they turned around,
They heard a rustle in the brush,
A sort of huffing sound,
My mother whispered to my aunt,
It's just one of the boys.
They think that they will scare us,
By making bearish noise,"
They talked a mile a minute,
And laughed aloud to show,
They weren't the slightest frightened,
The noise continued though,
It followed them into the yard,

But nothing could they see.
They were convinced it was the guys
Up to tomfoolery!
They grinned as they went in the door,
But those grins faded, when,
They saw a card game going on
And counted all the men!

Betty Lou Hebert

Photograph by Marilyn Califf

Sketch by Jane Mayfield

54

BULLFROG, BASS, LILY PAD

BULLFROG AND BASS SWIMMING IN A
STREAM
UP EARLY CAN'T WASTE TIME WHEN YOU
HAVE DREAMS
FROG TO BASS SAID I HAD A DREAM
OF BEING KISSED BY A PRINCESS AND
WAKING UP AS A KING

BASS TO FROG MY DREAM WAS NOT THAT
KIND
MY DREAM WAS GETTING CAUGHT ON A
LINE
PULLED FROM THE WATER TOOK AWAY FROM
MY HOME
TO HANG ON SOMEONE'S WALL THERE
HANGING ALL ALONE

SOMETIMES DREAMS DO COME TRUE
SO TRY TO DREAM THE DREAM THAT'S BEST
FOR YOU

FROG CLIMBED UP ON THE LILY PAD
EYES WIDE OPEN AND LOOKING SAD

BASS TO FROG, WHAT DO YOU SEE?
I SEE FIVE FAST BOATS AND I DON'T THINK
THEIR PRINCESS IS LOOKING FOR ME.

Larry D. Sutton

BALLET OF THE BUTTERFLY

A tiny angel
flirts with a beloved rose;
that is poesy.

Nature is enthralled
by the flying elegance
of this fantasy;

melancholic lakes
release their confined delight
with chaste ecstasy.

Rose petals are strung,
then written down on the grass
with affinity

like love poems filled
with imagery, redolent
with live vibrancy,

throbbing with pleasure
and eagerness, bringing back
a lost legacy.

Najwa Salam Brax

RESIDUE

She will be scrubbing the bathtub
quiet tears falling
on soap stains
on bloodstains
she will be thinking
my son   my sons
both of them

once in every two tears
she will sigh
my blind mother
feeling the vacancy in her womb
the barrenness in her heart
and she will continue
scrubbing
weeping
for she loves cleanliness
as she loved her sons

this is how I see it
this is how I see her life
on the morning of the night
                    mine ends.

Leonardo Alishan

ONIONS

make me cry--not the
lush purple Italians or sweet Vidalias--
slim, willowy ones, scallions up North,
but below the Mason-Dixon Line, green onions.

They're hardy--a must for any kitchen garden,
a must for someone who tills the soil
to know he's yet a man--still needed,
still defined by useful work
as my father was those final years.

In my back yard, he found a tiny sunny spot,
planted sets from his cousin's truck patch.
He weeded and loosened the soil
with a two-pronged cooking fork.

His onions cling to life now,
two summers since he left them--
tough, misshapen from their struggle,
nodding green tops heavy with sets.

Now my son is home, wounded by life and love.
He told a friend, "I'm back in the room
I had in high school, and
everything I own is in there with me."

He finds a tiny sunny spot, breaks ground,
turning over mounds of tradition,
looking for his roots.
Bending broad shoulders,
thrusting forward a slightly graying head,

he will place each heirloom set with care.
As I watch his shovel search for the courage

of his forebears, see him try to unearth
a reason to go on,
onions make me cry.

Marcia Camp

From *Voices International* and *Poems by Poets' Rountable of Arkansas* 1997

MORNING AS USUAL

When morning turns in the keyhole,
slithers between slats of the blinds,
flickers on the eyelids,
he wakes with feathered nose
to bacon frying
and customary coffee,
shaves off a sultan's dream
(but not close enough,)
kisses the cheek of aproned routine,
and, decrying the hours he would not forego
shrugs into the tailored coat of everyday
never guessing he would be naked without it.

Florence Holmes Ryan

From: from *Morning Turns In the Keyhole*, South & West, Inc. 1976

OBSTRUCTIONS

Insidious disease continues to bring
crises that further weaken the body
Through loss of strength, speech,
your very being

I reach out probing to touch
the fingers of your mind

You are here - yet you are not here.

I search your eyes for a bridge
to span the gap in understanding
to know what I can do to comfort
reassure you of the tensile strength
of the solid chord of love that binds us.

An inaudible whisper brings frustration.
Unable to grasp the message you are sending
I swallow hard to hold back the flow of tears
washing over my deepest emotions

Engulfed by tides of empty loneliness
grief wells up from my very depths
silken thread of life grows thinner

In my weariness I think
your suffering has been so long
I am ready for you to go - yet
I continue to cling
to each lucid moment

When clearly you say,
"I don't want to die."
I realize
letting go is painful
also for you.

Frances Darby

COLLISION ON THE PRODUCE AISLE

Your stunned tomatoes splattered into juice.
My wounded cherries bled across the floor.
We should be sensitive to such abuse
Of produce, and I'm sure you must deplore
My tactics, but your eyes are twice as blue
As berry cobbler cooling on a sill,
Your cheeks are peach-pink, and you are a true
Banana blonde; so now I hope you will
Forgive me. I am blushing-radish rude,
But overtures beside the cantaloupes
Do not come easy if I don't intrude.
You're glaring now, but still I have my hopes.
I saw a choice plum for a lonely heart.
That's why I swerved and crashed into your cart.

Russell Strauss

LEMON MOON

(A Dorsimbra)

I dreamed I waltzed across a lemon moon
And as I danced I saw you far away.
I smiled because I knew that very soon
We'd be together, dance all night, be gay.
The crash---
Head on---
I lived---
You died.
I mourned. I missed you terribly, but then
You came to me in dreams so very real.
I know we'll dance forever now because
I dreamed I waltzed across a lemon moon.

Patricia W. Smith

HAIKU

Wind whispers autumn
to blushing trees; leaves are coaxed
from summer's embrace.

Charles H. Johnson

62

Sunflowers - "Tapestry"

Photograph by Neal Hogenbirk

BUT SHELLS KEEP ON SINGING

In Memory of Jerry Leo Robbins

Like broken shells along the river bank
his dreams were dashed against the stormy night.
As illness froze his body, power sank--
Yet his poetic soul could still take flight!
April promises
melted
into
December ice.
But memories of him still come to mind
like mockingbirds that sing on lonely days
reflecting joys of vigoroso tides
like broken shells along the river bank.

Frances Brinkley Cowden

HAIKU

A full moon floats just
above the treetops -- a pearl
on emerald seas.

Charles H. Johnson

ALICE JOY

Florence Bruce

In dreams I'm still enchanted by the unforgettable voice of my Uncle Earl, who worked in radio. He was invited to our house for Christmas dinner the year his wife Emma -- my mother's sister -- died in August. He arrived with two beautifully wrapped packages, one for me and one for my older sister Christine. One box looked like it might contain houseshoes, and the other was big enough to hold anything -- a winter coat or a wonderful game. I wanted the big one.

It was a wartime Christmas in the forties -- overall, a miserable Christmas. My father and my uncle were scarcely acquainted, and in fact, had nothing in common. Hence, they danced politely around each other, talking about safe subjects like the weather and Mr. Roosevelt, who, all seemed agreed, was second only to God.

Finally, Father allowed Christine and me to open our presents from Uncle Earl. My sister went first, opening the big box. Father became visibly upset when he beheld its contents -- a maroon velvet suit. He felt it highly improper for an uncle by marriage to give clothing to his unmarried daughter of sixteen. By some miracle, however, father held his tongue and his temper, and the moment passed, for which I heard my mother sigh in relief.

Then I opened my gift. From the smaller box lined with tissue, I delivered the loveliest doll I had ever seen. Her brown hair was real. Her costume was pale yellow with a hat to match. Her dress was adorned with tiny velvet flowers of pink, blue and purple. Her shoes and socks were removable. She carried a staff in one hand and wore a tag which read "Little Bo Peep."

"Guess you'll name her Bo Peep," my uncle said.

My mother, no doubt to please him and to preserve her sister's memory, said, "You could name her Emma Loraine." She paused waiting for my response. "Or Alice Joy after Emma's daughter, your cousin. What do you say?"

"Alice Joy," I intoned. "It's beautiful like she is."

Before another Christmas came, my mother had died also. No one comforted me or explained her death. My father simply could not handle emotional things and made no effort.

The doll my grief-stricken uncle had given me in 1941 provided a means for me to deal with the profound grief associated with losing my mother in childhood. I sat under the magnolia tree in my grandmother's yard and made clothes for my lovely doll, Alice Joy. I poured my heart out to her, my grief. The look in her lovely blue eyes, the sympathy I read in her face, told me someone understood and cared. I propped her up with her arms outstretched, and pretended she was hurrying forward to comfort me. With Alice Joy for my audience, I practiced before the mirror in my bedroom until I could say aloud, without tears, "My mother is dead."

A few years later, I overheard my grandmother talking on the phone about a black child named Canary, who lived in the alley behind her house. By report, the child's mother had been killed, and she would be taken to live with her aged grandmother. I walked across my grandmother's back yard to the fence that separated it from the alley, and called aloud,

"Canary! Canary!"

I handed Alice Joy and a shoebox full of doll clothes over the fence to her. I was getting too old to play with dolls anyhow.

MRS. O'HALLORAN'S GARDEN

Reese Danley-Kilgo

Mrs. O'Halloran was always in her garden before sunrise. Early morning joggers looked for her, slowed down, waved. She sat on her front steps drinking a cup of lemon-balm tea -- she grew her own herbs -- until it grew light enough to work.

This morning she almost dropped her cup.

"I could have sworn there were just two rosebushes there last night! My Chicago Peace and my Queen Elizabeth -- I pruned them--"

They were there, one on each side of the steps, blooming profusely, perfectly pruned. But stretching from the steps down the walk were twenty other rosebushes, pinks, whites, yellows. Mrs. O'Halloran didn't care for red roses. She recognized a few favorites, John F. Kennedy, King's Ransom, First Prize. She looked down the walk, couldn't believe her eyes. Nor her nose. She reached out to touch silvery pink petals, bent slowly to smell the heady perfume of Jadis, one of the few early hybrid teas that kept its old-fashioned fragrance.

"I had one of those--" She couldn't remember when, or what had happened to it. She walked slowly, touching a petal here, a leaf there. At the end she turned, looked back at the garden, the house. The fresh white paint was dazzling, the green shutters shiny in the rising sun. The dogwood tree, leafy now in May, shaded an encircling bed of green and white hosta. Late azaleas, white, lavender, watermelon-pink, bloomed near the house. Drops of dew sparkled on the green patch of lawn, neatly mowed, edged.

Mrs. O'Halloran remembered the feel of bare feet in wet grass. She sat on the steps, tugged at her garden boots, finally removed one. The other was more difficult. She couldn't seem to get it into her hands and pull her foot out at the same time.

"Must have shrunk," she said aloud. She smiled at the idea of a rubber boot shrinking. When she finally got it off, she held onto the rail to pull herself up, stood a minute regaining her balance, walked slowly around the rosebushes to the small lawn. Wading through the grass, she thought of her mother, of herself as a small child. "Walking barefoot in dew will give you ground-itch," her mother had said, but let her do it anyway, then dried each toe carefully with a rough white towel, put her socks and sandals back on. The sandals were scuffed brown leather, T-strapped, round-toed.

The wet grass felt cool to Mrs. O'Halloran's feet. She decided to sit down, tried to bend, almost fell, finally made it. Smoothing the grass with both hands, she sat listening to a mockingbird singing high in the pecan tree, sang a phrase with him: "Oh, what is so rare as a morning in May..." She thought, not quite the words, but they fit anyway.

Looking up with a start when a car stopped at her gate, Mrs. O'Halloran said, "Now who in the world could that be? Was I expecting somebody?" She didn't know the middle-aged man who got out, came toward her. Closer, he looked somehow familiar, reminding her of someone she knew.

"Good Lord, Mother, what are you doing sitting out here on the wet grass?"

At his exasperated half-smile and the way he said "Mother," Mrs. O'Halloran suddenly recognized her son. But he looks so old, she thought. Patrick is not that old. Look at all that gray in his hair, and in his beard, too!

"Good Lord yourself, Patrick," she said, smiling up at him. "I'm just sitting here enjoying the morning! What are you doing here so early?"

"Mom, remember? I've come to take you over to the apartment. You're moving, remember?"

68

The patience in his earnest voice, the pain on his face, made Mrs. O'Halloran want to comfort Patrick and shake him at the same time. My memory loss hurts him more than it does me, she thought. It's just a confounded nuisance. She thought hard, couldn't remember a thing about an apartment.

"What apartment?" she finally asked. "Now why would I move to an apartment?"

"Camellia Complex," he said. "You remember? You liked the apartment, the skylight in the bathroom, we hung all those baskets of plants..."

Suddenly she remembered that bathroom, blue and white tiles, a skylight --- she loved it. She and Patrick had filled it with hanging baskets of philodendron and maidenhair ferns, set African violets by the lavatory. They had put small pots of herbs on the kitchen windowsill over the tiny sink.

"It's an 'assisted living' place, Mom. You remember, you need more help now, and there they--"

"Okay, Patrick, I remember now. And you're right, I need all the help I can get. So give me a hand to get up off this wet lawn," she commanded. "Hard getting down, but a darn sight harder getting up!" She held out both hands toward him.

Patrick bent down, put his arms around her shoulders, helped her to her feet, walked her toward the car. Settling her gently in the front seat, fastening her seat belt, he said, "Wait here a minute, I'll be right back."

He went up the walk, looked at the two straggly rosebushes. He bent and broke off the last two blooms. They would look good in the crystal vase on his mother's new coffee table. He remembered giving the vase to his mother the Christmas he was ten. Sudden tears stinging his eyes, he looked around at the house, at the yard, picked up a pair of pruning shears rusting in the grass. He thought, I have to remember to call the real estate agency. This place needs a lot of painting and yard work before it's put up for sale.

At the car he handed the two roses to his mother. She smiled at him. Who is this middle-aged man, she thought. He looks familiar, and he's giving me roses, so it must be all right to go with him.

"That's a Queen Elizabeth and a Chicago Peace," she said.

Photograph by Frances Darby

TOO LATE TOMORROW

Hollis K. Cathey

My breathing came hard as my heart pounded in my chest. I knew I had to rest soon, even if IT caught up to me again. I couldn't go faster, not with the rags I had earlier this morning found and tied around both feet. I stopped under a leafless oak and sank against its trunk. Slowly I lifted a foot and looked at the spots of red seeping through the cloth.

Oh, how I wished for a pair of leather shoes, or shoes of any kind. But that would never happen again. As far as I knew, there were no longer any cows left alive on earth and from what I had been able to learn, there were not many animals of any kind living, especially the soft human animal.

How could this all happen? I was born at the turn of the century and this is the year 2050. During my lifetime peace and prosperity reigned. War was almost a thing of the past. Industry flourished and people were happy, and then a year ago, or was it two, things drastically changed. What the psalm singers and "Green" people preached about had happened.

What was the name they used? Oh yes, Tree Death Syndrome and they had another word for it, walsterben. When it suddenly hit with its ominous fury, forest and grasslands across the globe died within a very short time. They said Mother Nature, tired of holding back, unleashed her wrath and extracted her penalties of death world wide.

Cities and even whole countries were laid to waste. Food and water began to be rationed, but finally that bit of organization played out, and it was every person for himself. This blight upon us became so bad that people would kill for a mouthful of good clean water or something safe to eat.

In the beginning of this holocaust they said I was one of those to blame. Me! All I did was serve my fellow man. Didn't I build large industrial complexes that employed thousands of people? Sure, I may have cut corners on pollution control as they said, but it was only so I could build more plants and hire more people.

And haven't I paid a hard price? My family is all gone now. I alone survive. They should have known I wouldn't have done this to my loved ones. But I fooled them--well, almost. Before the aircraft stopped flying, the TV stations went off the air and all but a few radio stations stopped broadcasting, I brought my wife and daughter to Alaska.

I thought there would always be water to drink and game to eat here, but I was wrong. Now, most everything is poisoned and the forests of Southern Alaska are almost a desert. I've had to go farther north to escape the terrible heat. The ice cap is rapidly melting and the land is shrinking because of this thing we called global warming. Tremors are felt daily, but I will survive. I must! If only I could hear another human voice. Yesterday my last radio battery went dead. Now I am indeed alone.

Wait! I hobble to my tender feet and cock my head to the side, listening. What is this I hear? I raise my nose and sniff the air. Oh, no! The smell, the sound! IT is coming toward me! I must hurry to my cave. I can't be caught again. I barely survived the last time, I run, trying to ignore my pained bloody feet, I can't forget the stinging, blistering torture that felt as if burning needles were jabbing my body or the loss of one eye from the encounter.

Hurry! Hurry! I sense the thing is close now. Another few yards and I'll be safe. I stumble and fall then try to rise, but I am weak. I struggle on, even though I feel the burning needles again. IT is upon me. This horrible IT ... Acid rain!

Was I--was mankind to blame for this? No matter. Too late now. The droplets cover me and I feel the sharp-- wait! "O Death, where is thy sting? ..."* That phrase flashes through my mind, for I feel no pain from the horrid rain. I stop and cup my palms together and they fill with the liquid. I drink and the taste is sweet. I raise my arms toward the heavens and shout praises to the Lord, then turn and walk into my cave. I sit against the wall and watch outside as the sweet nectar flows, and I think.

* I Corinthians 15:55 (KJV)

HAIKU

Black spider dances,
Tracing a gossamer path
To spin her partner.

Diane M. Clark

LETTER TO THE EDITOR

Lucille Bogue

Thank you for bringing us the news, even though it some times makes us sick to read it. As does the story on clear-cutting in the Routt National Forest. I simply couldn't believe it! I knew that the ruthless big lumber companies did that sort of thing, here in California -- but not in Routt and Medicine Bow! Not in our precious, pristine home forests.

It is a personal blow to my ideals. During WWII, my husband was a forest ranger with Routt National Forest, a job we both felt was a noble profession, the protection of our God-given forests. For two years we lived in the Columbine Ranger Station with our two little girls, Sharon and Bonnie, and all of us dearly loved the forests that surrounded us.

Art's job was to ride the range and keep track of the great flocks of sheep that moved through, so that they would keep moving and not overgraze and harm the forests. Another part of his job in protecting our hallowed forests was that of acting as fire-lookout in the tiny station atop Hahns Peak during times of high fire danger.

Many is the time I have ridden up across those great tumbled boulders to the summit to do day-long fire duty, with four-year-old Bonnie clinging with terrified tenacity to the back of my saddle, while Sharon, six, clung to Art's. And for what? Risking our lives to save the forests for the plundering lumber industry? I can't believe this is happening!

I cannot blame the local forest service, for they are just carrying out the orders of our national government, I suppose. But can none of those in authority see farther than their noses -- not even as far as tomorrow? It doesn't take

74

anyone trained in forestry to realize that those vast expanses of clear-cut forests that not long ago blanketed our northern Rockies, now shaved clean by the rapists, leave the naked earth exposed to devastating erosion.

And this erosion is carried by mountain thunderstorms and melting winter snows down into our creeks and rivers, destroying our fishing streams for years to come with the run-off of top soil along with the ability of our woods to ever live again. It will take hundreds of years for Routt Forest to recover it original health and vitality -- if ever! Naked mountains -- and valleys of mud! Our children's inheritance.

One of the most appalling aspects of this ruthless destruction of our forests was the sneaking and dishonest manner in which it was perpetrated, keeping the public, the owners of our forestland, America, you and me -- in the dark until the published air photographs uncovered this clandestine annihilation. The forest service allowed this wanton demolition only out of sight of the mountain roads which crisscross the Rockies. It wasn't until you published the air-photos taken by Bio-diversity Associates that the public had any concept of this immoral and overwhelming destruction of our forest-clad mountains. And to think our honored forest service is responsible!

Bio-diversity's photos leave me chilled to the bone. I can't believe those naked and ragged mountains are the identical mountains that Art spent years cherishing and watch-dogging. How could America allow this violent destruction of our Earth and its rich resources? I can agree that people need homes and the lumber with which to construct them. But why this wanton clear-cutting?

When I read your article revealing this scandalous atrocity and stared, disbelieving, at the hideous results in the photos, I felt I was viewing the devastation and rape of the wooded mountains of Tibet, after the ruthless and greedy Chinese had finished their plunder. The Tibetans

75

have now fled their naked and flood-harrassed homeland. It is no longer possible to live on their own piece of denuded Earth. Are Americans copy-catting the Chinese? Do we care about our own children?

It is possible, you know, to lumber "selectively," cutting only mature trees out of a stand and leaving only the half-grown or those that are as yet not ready for harvest, thus protecting the humus, the dark top soil resulting from the decomposition of plant and animal matter so essential to the fecundity of the Earth. Clear cutting allows this to be washed out to sea, thus contaminating our oceans, while at the same time destroying our land. This "mud," as we call it after being mixed with river water, settles to the bottom of the oceans, burying and destroying deep-sea life, such as coral, sea anemones, sea urchins and myriads of other fragile forms of sea life. How can professionals, supposedly educated to protect our forests, be a part of this wholesale slaughter of our Earth?

Of course, lumber tycoons don't approve selective harvesting for producing lumber. Too costly, they say. Cut clean, cut as fast as you can, then, move on. And fast. Don't waste any time worrying about the sentimental "tree huggers." We're in this business to make money. This is one business where they give us the forests, so it's only common sense to cut as fast and cheaply as possible -- then skedaddle! Forget the homeless wild animals!

Oh, yes they promise to replant before they leave for their winter homes in the Bahamas. And they do. Usually. But what kind of an environment do those poor delicate little seedlings find themselves in? Eroded mountains, top soil washed away, whipped by winter blizzards and without the protection and shade needed from burning summer sun. How many will survive?

And how many centuries will it take these few survivors, if there are any, to propagate a full and vital forest, the kind we used to guard from the hazardous top of Hahns Peak? Three or four hundred years, at least.

I don't ever want to look out across the verdant expanse of Colorado forests again. I couldn't bear the anguish, knowing I was seeing only the naked bleached bones of the forest I once knew and cherished. Now there are only scraggly patches of trees, retained to deceive the passing public and to cover the theft.

Art, I am glad you aren't here to see what they've done to your forest. A noble profession, indeed!

Dear Editor, thank you for bringing us the news, even though it makes us sick to read it.

§§§

SUNRISE

Sense the peace of sunrise...
sneaking softly,
in slippered whispers.
Snaking through stillness
arousing us slowly
from slumber.

Tammy D. Moon

GIFTS

Reese Danley-Kilgo

It is an important day. I want to give you something.
"No gift," you say. Your put your arms around me,
your voice muffled in my shoulder. "I have everything I
want right here."
I hold you close, smooth your hair. It is white and
thin as dandelion fluff. It still feels thick and silky to me.
Now sitting at my desk, I think of how your hair
feels under my fingers. I try to think of a present. I turn on
my word processor. Retired from a life time of teaching, I
want to be a writer, a novelist. As always you encourage me,
give me hope. Gave me this word processor, a gift for
retirement, said, "Okay, now be a writer."
Today the novel will have to wait. I sit here and
think of you. It is an important day. I want to give you
something.
. . . .
"Yes," you said, and smiled. "Yes."
That one word made my life, the path I've followed,
my destiny. Not many people can pinpoint the very
moment, the exact words, the actual time and place when
their lives change, never again to be the same. The sharp turn
in the road, the new direction.
But I can. I have only to close my eyes to see it all.
The green hill, the dark pines in the field, the sea beyond.
The waves are coming in slowly, breaking to sudsy foam on
the white sand. We walk on the narrow strip of beach,
patterned by brown seaweed drying in the sun. It smells
salty, faintly fishy.
"You will?" I ask. I couldn't believe you said yes. I
had hoped, but never really believed it would happen. I had
not planned to ask you then. It was a spring day, 1945.

What did I have to offer you? A five-year struggle on the GI Bill.

I know it was harder on you than on me. But we did it, didn't we? And enjoyed it. Went through college, had two children, a second-hand crib, no baby bathtub. We bathed them in the sink. Splash, splatter, life and laughter. Apartment so small we used the kitchen table for a desk, typed our term papers there.

Then the offer of a graduate assistantship and three more years of living in student housing, old army barracks under the Florida pines. I couldn't ask you to continue living like that. Could I?

"Yes," you say.

. . . .

All my life you have given me everything. What can I give you today? I sit here at this desk, trying to think of something. I want to finish the novel. For you. Your belief in me, your pride in my accomplishments.

Write in scenes, the "How to Write" books say. Show scenes in which your characters develop the plot, move the action forward. Sometimes I can do that. But not today.

I can't look forward. Only back, over my life. Scene after scene. You are the central character in them all.

. . . . . .

"It's so green," you say.

"All this rain," I say grumpily, damply. "No wonder."

But the sun comes out in Donegal as we drive south to County Clare. You love the thorny hedgerows, narrow little roads winding over round hills, white sheep grazing in green fields. They come up and stare at us curiously. I offer one a pickle from our picnic basket. You laugh.

The sheep have red splotches of dye on their backs. We are mystified, ask a passing farmer in a cart. The cart is half-filled with squares of dark peat.

"For identification.." he says.

79

"I like your sweater," you tell him.

His sweater is heavy, creamy wool, knitted in a design of squares and ridges. I want to buy you one like it in the airport shop. You won't let me, say it's too expensive, we've already spent too much for this vacation.

"But you're glad we came?" I ask, needing your reassurance, as always. We hold hands, walking through the airport. The signs are written in Gaelic and English.

"Yes," you say, and smile.

. . . .

I take out the half-filled box of manuscript. I read the last chapter, mid-way, unfinished. Will I ever finish it? I haven't looked at it for four months. I don't want it to end.

A mockingbird sings in the pecan tree outside my study window. The daffodils are pushing up green spikes through the brown leaf mulch we raked over the beds last fall. The forsythia you planted years ago, thin switches then, are big bushes now, blooming by the fence.

Spring is unbearably beautiful.

Unbearable.

. . . .

In January the weather was cold. Southern winters sometimes have warm spells, but not this year.

We drove home from the office in shock. I have no memory of the drive back, until we are in the kitchen. The kitchen we painted, yellow with white trim. I look at the Blue Willow plates you hung over the window, around the wall to the door. The lab report lies on the table between us.

"It's not true," I say. "There has to be some mistake."

You shake your head. I know there is no mistake.

"But nothing is definite," I say. "There's always hope. We'll do everything! We'll fight this, won't we?"

"Yes," you say.

. . . . . .

We have. And we may win.

80

We have made it through the gray winter.

Today is an important day. I sit here at my desk and try to think of a gift for you. The gift I want to give you is life. I know I can't.

I put the manuscript back in the box, and look in the desk drawer for scissors. I'm going out to cut yellow forsythia for the blue vase by your bed.

The novel will have to wait.

§§

BEHOLD

God pressed a buton
  and gave the ginkgo one hour
to shed every leaf.

Towering above the housetop
  a golden treasure trove
it stood in beauty bound.

Then as if each leaf said, "It's time!"
  magically the race began
leaf on leaf, they steadily fell.

Joining up as they collided
  they stacked the ground below
returning the gold to earth.

Bare branches await
  the resurrection of Spring--
Behold the hand of God!

Louise Hays

DANIEL

Martha McNatt

When Daniel was born, thirty-seven years ago in the Upper Midwest, his parents received devastating news. "Your baby is severely handicapped," their doctors told them. "He will never speak or walk. He will never even smile. Our advice to you is to find a place for institutional care, and try to forget he was ever born."

His parents, Len and Norma were unable to accept the cruel advice. Knowing they were making a lifetime commitment, they determined that with God's help, they would give their baby loving care. They would help him to develop to whatever extent possible, and they would accept him as a member of the family.

At the time of his birth, Daniel's deficiency was known as Mongolism (now known as Down Syndrome). Beginning the day they took him home, Norma began to read everything available concerning his condition; how it was perceived by physicians, educators, and the general public. They sought medical specialists, education professionals, therapists--anyone who might help with the task ahead.

Response was discouraging. One physician told them that Mongoloid Children made nice house pets, but never became real family members. An education specialist told them that in school he might be taught to button his coat, handle his bathroom habits, and eat with a spoon but little else. They were warned of dire physical conditions he would encounter, including premature aging, arthritis, and visual deterioration.

His parents refused to be discouraged. Daniel was learning to sit, stand and smile. He responded to voices and to colors. With the help of a specialized educational system, Norma developed an individualized educational plan for her child. When he was a toddler, Norma began to stimulate him with color. She handed him a red ball and said the words "red ball." She handed him a yellow ball and said the words "yellow ball." Thousands of repetitions later, she handed him the red ball and said, "What is this?"

The day he responded, "red ball,"was the happiest day of our lives." said Norma.

Norma and Len reached out to other parents of Down Syndrome children. Together, parents organized a school with an individualized program for each child, with guidance from Norma. As many as fifty children and parents at the time, were involved in the school.

Gradually Daniel developed the skills they had been told were impossible for him. He learned to walk and speak, read a little, and to count money. As a young teen, Daniel had a paper route, which he could manage with some help from Dad. Later he worked as a grocery bag boy, and on the clean up crew of another business. Daniel experienced job prejudices, and hurt feelings from unkind remarks made by uncaring persons, but he did not give up. He just tried for another job.

As public awareness increased, federal funds became available for training handicapped children and adults. With the passage of P.L. 94122, which stated that handicapped children have a right to free and equal public education, opportunities skyrocketed, and so did Daniel. He spent six years in a group home where he learned life and occupational skills. He developed a love for music and seemed to manage the trappings of electronic musical devices.

At age thirty-seven, Daniel lives at home with his parents, and attends a work program for developmentally disadvantaged adults. He holds two jobs at the center, for which he is paid a decent wage. His room is decorated with pictures of Jesus and a statue of the Virgin Mary. "He always wears a cross around his neck when we go to Church," said Norma. "He loves Bible stories about Jesus and he enjoys singing hymns, both at home and at Church." He suffers none of the health horror stories his parents were warned about.

Daniel has a girl friend who works alongside him at the Center. They spend much of the time they are apart with an open phone line, talking and listening to music together. They want to get married. Both sets of parents have agreed that if their relationship continues for two years, the marriage may occur. Supervised living apartments are available for handicapped couples within the program in which they now participate.

"God has been in our lives all the way," said Norma. "Daniel is truly our miracle child, and our lives have been blessed beyond measure."

§§§

HAIKU

Even an empty
heart remembers in the dusk
there. was once an "us"

LaVonne Schoneman

THE FLIGHT HOME

Anne H. Norris

Trudging along toward Gate 36 with a bag of San Francisco sourdough bread in one hand, attaché case in the other, and raincoat over my arm, I wondered why my flight seemed to always depart from the farthest gate. I was in pain. My head ached. My feet hurt. Parts in between felt like I had been hit by a runaway cable car.

San Francisco is a wonderful city, but a four-day convention there can do terrible things to one's body. I was ready for Memphis and a quiet weekend at home.

I could see a crowd at the distant gate. The flight would be full if not overbooked. I wouldn't volunteer to give up my seat for a round-trip ticket to Paris. I wanted to board the plane, get settled into my reserved aisle seat, and sleep all the way home.

I eased into the long line with a sigh of relief that boarding was underway. I returned the flight attendant's greeting, but my forced smile lasted only a minute. In my aisle seat was a grandmotherly-looking lady, buckled in for the flight. I suggested she move next to the window, explaining that she was in my seat. "No," she said, "This is where they told me to sit." She had no intention of moving.

I had no intention of giving up my aisle seat. Bucking the oncoming passengers, I solicited help from the flight attendant whose smile was beginning to fade.

It was with reluctance that the lady finally moved. The flight attendant had explained that she now could look out the window. That was not a good selling point. She did not want to look out, feeling this would make her air sick when we took off. She asked me to let her know when we were in the air. I promised I would.

I closed my eyes, hoping for peace and quiet. Not to be had. The lady informed me she had gone to California on a bus to visit her son. She had sprained her ankle and the doctor felt it would be advisable for her to fly back. This was her first time on a plane.

Our delay in taking off was explained by one of the flight attendants. I had to repeat her message to the lady beside me. "One of the toilets is out of order," I said," and since the plane is fully loaded and the flight will be several hours, it will have to be repaired before we can leave."

She shrugged her shoulders and said loudly, "I wasn't planning to use the toilet before we get to Memphis anyway." Passengers around us were smiling. The fun had only begun!

Faithful to my promise, I informed the lady when finally we were airborne. "Are we going to have a movie now?" she asked.

"No, Ma'm, movies are shown only on the big planes," I said.

"But isn't this a big plane?" she asked.

I explained that the plane was small compared to jumbo jets. Moreover it did not have a screen for showing movies.

Fumbling with her seat belt, she sought my assistance in unbuckling it. She didn't want to go anywhere. She just didn't want the seat belt fastened. I explained the airline policy that passengers are asked to keep their seat belts fastened as a safety precaution in the event turbulent weather is encountered. She looked at me and then at passengers walking toward the rear of the plane. "Where are those people going?" she asked.

"Probably to the rest room," I replied, wondering why she couldn't figure that out herself.

"Well," she said very matter-of-factly, "I guess they have their seat belts unfastened." I leaned over and released the buckle.

Choosing her entree at meal time needed my assistance. Should she have baked chicken or lasagna? She didn't want anything that might upset her stomach. I agreed, suggesting the chicken ... for both of us. Although I preferred lasagna, I had a feeling if I got lasagna and she got chicken, she would want to trade.

"Why are we flying along the highway," was her next question. At her insistence, I leaned over to look. I never convinced her she was seeing the wing of our plane.

I welcomed the announcement that we were in the approach pattern for Memphis, although the flight had not been boring. A flight attendant walked back, holding forth a bottle of champagne for my seat companion.

"For you," she said, "to celebrate your first plane ride." I attempted to explain that it was a gift from the airline.

Her comment was emphatic, "I don't drink."

As soon as we landed and the seat belt sign was off, the lady was standing. Leaning impatiently on the back of the seat in front of her, looking over the shoulder of the gentleman still seated there, she declared loudly enough to be heard by those in the rear of the plane, "This man just had his first flight too."

I could feel eyes turning our way as I asked how she came by this information. "Because he's got a bottle of champagne," she informed me, as well as all the other passengers.

This was too much. I peered over the seat to see the bottle of champagne for myself. The man whose ears now were turning from pink to red did not have a bottle of champagne. What he had was a folding umbrella, with the handle upturned.

Passengers were beginning to move forward. I stepped into the aisle and made room ahead of me for the lady. I knew why the other passengers were smiling. They had enjoyed the in-flight entertainment.

The entire crew was lined up at the front of the plane. As I approached the door, one of the flight attendants reached out to present me with a bottle of champagne.
"This is for you, with our appreciation. You deserve it."

Unlike my seat companion, I readily accepted the gift.

§§§

Time, March 10, 1998, "A Sheep Named Dolly," Dr. Ian Wilmut took the nucleus of a cell from the udder of a six-year-old ewe and fashioned from it a perfect clone, then plungled in an electric charger to get it growing.

HELLO, DOLLY

From the udder of a six-year-old ewe
came a cell he thought would do.

As he plunged the electric charger in,
cloning Dolly, the perfect twin,

Doctor Wilmut was heard to utter
"She's the offspring of a significant udder."

Helen F. Blackshear

SENT BY GOD

Rosemary Stephens

My husband and I had been visiting his parents in New Jersey and were on our way home to Florida, when an unforgettable incident occurred in our lives.

I had fallen asleep in the car after lunch, and when I awoke, we were surrounded by whiteness. "Did it snow? Oh, it's cotton!" I exclaimed. Cotton fields as far as we could see to the right, left, behind us and in front of the car, lining the road, covering the entire earth. "We aren't on the main highway, are we?"

"This is a short cut," my husband said. "The cashier at the restaurant said it would take about thirty miles off our trip."

"It's lovely, but lonely," I observed.

"A couple of cars passed us before you woke up. This is a state road that cuts through some big cotton farms. Hey, what's that?" Our car swerved and we both heard a kind of clunking noise. Then the engine turned off as he guided the car over to the shoulder of the road. "Maybe we're out of gas," he said.

"We got gas before lunch," I pointed out. Surely our gas tank wasn't leaking. The car was only a couple of years old. My husband knew nothing about motors. He had never fooled about with cars the way my father and brother had done, for my husband had always had a good mechanic whom he trusted.

After raising the hood, he stared at the engine for a few minutes, then poked about with a stick for several more minutes. Shrugging, he checked the gas tank. Then, returning to the car window, he said, "I don't know what's wrong."

A car whizzed past us.

"Flag down the next car," I suggested. "They can send a mechanic from the nearest garage."

Twenty minutes later, there was a next car, and it too sailed by. Half an hour later, a car from the opposite direction also failed to stop. Then I noticed a house just beyond the field to our right. We could see a chimney and part of a roof. "Maybe they have a phone," I said.

"It would take at least an hour to walk there and back. I'd rather try to stop a car," he grumbled.

No cars. Then I cried, "Look! Something's coming!"

Moving toward us on the edge of the road was an old farm wagon pulled by a mule. As it got closer, we saw that the driver was a man wearing farm clothes. "Maybe he works around here," I said. "Or lives over there," my husband suggested. We had not even noticed the dirt road that cut through the field toward the distant house until the man turned the wagon into it. He stopped the mule and just sat there, looking at us.

"Thank God you're here," my husband called to him. "Do you know anything about motors? My car won't start. Is there a phone in that house? Can you give me a hand?"

The man said nothing. He seemed to be studying my husband, then our car, then me, for I was getting out of the car, pulling on my fur jacket against the cool air. Then the man looked up and down the road and across the vast fields.

At that moment his eyes locked with mine. My blood seemed to scream, "Danger!" He's going to rob us, I realized. But he flicked the mule with his whip and the wagon began to move onto the dirt road.

"Will you come back and help me?" my husband called. The man looked back at him, gave a quick nod, and the wagon went on.

"Nothing to worry about now," my husband said with relief. "If he has a phone, he'll call a garage. Anyway, he'll be back soon."

"What's the matter with you?" I said. "That man is not going to help anybody!"

"Nonsense, he'll be back, you'll see."

I said nothing. The wind grew colder and I returned to sit in the car. My husband stood beside it, watching the road. There were no more cars. After about an hour, he said, "Here he comes now. I told you."

Now there were two men in the wagon. As they came closer, I saw the guns. The second man was holding a long shotgun across his lap. The driver had placed another gun so it leaned against him, beside the seat.

I closed my eyes. "Oh, God, please help us!" I prayed silently.

"These are evil men -- I know it. Please help us. Send somebody, please. Don't let them kill us!"

I was trembling so badly I could not move. My eyes were open now. The wagon still had a bit of ground to cover before it would reach us. "Listen," I said, intending to warn my husband, but he was saying, "I knew he'd help us."

Just then something swerved around us and brakes squealed in front of our car. A tremendous truck materialized before our eyes. We had not heard it coming. It had a lot of very big tires beneath it, and it was hauling Texaco gasoline.

A very tall driver stepped down from the truck's cab. "You folks need some help?" he asked.

My husband told him what had happened, and the young man said, "Let me take a look."

"Oh, God, thank you, thank you!" I whispered. I was finally able to move, and I got out of the car. The

91

wagon had stopped when the truck pulled over. I could see the faces of both men clearly now, and I was terrified. But I still clung to hope and trust in God.

The wagon driver dropped the reins and reached for his gun, but the other one grabbed his arm, and said something in a low growling voice.

"Thank you for your help!" I called. "But this man has everything under control. We appreciate your kindness, but we don't need your help any more. Thanks again."

Both men looked at me. Their bodies were like zombies, but their eyes were wary and chilling. They whispered to each other, then the driver turned the mule and they went slowly back through the cotton field. Halfway to the house, they stopped the wagon again, and sat there, looking back at us as if waiting for something.

I knew they were waiting for the truck driver to leave. When he can't fix it, he'll leave and they'll come back, I thought. I knew they would rob us, kill my husband, and, finally, murder me.

"Please, God, please," I repeated like a litany. "Please."

"That ought to do it," the young man told my husband. "Try it now."

The car started on the third try and I burst into tears. My husband offered to pay the trucker, but he refused with a smile.

"There are several gas stations this side of Raleigh," he said. "One of them is the station I service. They've got a good mechanic. Tell him Mike sent you. He'll fix your fan belt and replace the distributor."

I walked with him over to the cab of his truck. "Please do one last favor for us," I said. "Be sure we get the car going on the road ahead of you so that you can see everything is all right. I'm afraid those two men might come back before we can really get away from here."

"Sure thing," he said.

So we finally left, with the big truck following us. After a bit, it passed us, the horn blasting away. We followed it for miles. Cotton fields gave way to trees, grass, houses, and stores. The road took a big turn and the truck disappeared from our sight. After we made the turn, the road straightened again.

"Where did he go?" my husband muttered.

"He just -- vanished," I said.

We looked carefully but there was no crossroad, and he had not parked in any of the driveways or store lots.

An hour later, we saw the Texaco station, and my husband pulled in.

When he finished talking to the mechanic, I told the man, "A Texaco driver named Mike told us to stop here. Do you know him?"

"Sure do," he grinned. "Great guy. He delivers gas here every Thursday. Nice fellow."

Today was Monday. I knew then that God had sent us a miracle. A guardian angel named Michael is in the Bible. Maybe a whole troop of angels are named Michael. Or did God pluck a very kind, ordinary man out of time just long enough to save our lives?

I've always believed he was really an angel, sent by God in answer to my prayer.

Reprinted from: *Angels, Messengers of Love and Grace,* Life Press, 1999

ANEMONES
Elizabeth Howard
Grandmother Earth, $8.95, Paper

Reviewd by Patricia W. Smith

My reaction after the first reading of this slim volume of poems (pre-publication, proof copy) was "Wow!" I felt that I had had a glimpse of the author's soul and wished that I could write like that. Poignant, heart-wrenching, gentle, historic are all words that come to mind about Mrs. Howard's poetry. In "The Foot-Washing": "She washed his feet, great-grandmother/kneeling before great-grandfather ... but the hands/talking love the way words never had."

Howard lives in Crossville, Tennessee, where she has been writing seriously for ten years and has had over four hundred pieces published in over eighty journals and anthologies. Every poem in this book has been previously published. Among her awards was 1996 Writer of the Year presented by the Cookeville Creative Writers Association in Cookeville, Tennessee.

Included in the book is an unusual poem about wife abuse and one about the effect a teenaged girl's death had on those who knew her. But it is not all gloomy. In "Heron Mosaic" a successful fishing trip is remembered and "Earthworks" tells of a visit to a field on Cumberland Gap where "soldiers waited weary months/for 'the battle that never came.'/ ... The rattle of arms has given way/to the rustle of autumn leaves./whispering of peace and beauty."

THORNS TO VELVET

Blanche S. Boren
Life Press, Frances Brinkley Cowden, Editor
Hardback, $19.95

Reviewed by Frances Darby

Thorns to Velvet reveals a life-long journey of faith compressed into 174 pages. The book of devotionals carries a positive message of strength, character, courage, and service.

Boren had known and faced the thorns of life, not only to survive while coping with disappointments and sorrows, also to appreciate the beauty of roses and inhale the lovely fragrance of love and happiness. She explains how she learned about God as a child while working with her grandmother in her rose garden. "I learned to love roses even when I questioned why they had thorns." Her grandmother with whom she lived as a child following the death of Boren's mother taught her to spend time alone with God in prayer and to read and study His word.

In the section, "Do Not Be Afraid," Boren says,"God is with us in times of need to give peace and comfort even when we are not aware of His presence." Through her reflections, she shares both the thorns and the roses and how family, friends and even chance acquaintances have given her insight into God's plan for her life. She invites the reader to share in this journey of faith.

Grandmother Earth's Healthy and Wise Cookbook

Barbara Abbott, Editor
Grandmother Earth, $14.95

Reviewed by Patricia W. Smith

This small (192 pages) but comprehensive cookbook is edited by Barbara Britton Abbott, It features southern cooking in a healthier mode. Many recipes were chosen for their ease of preparation.

Included in the book are samples of recipes from five generations of the publisher/contributing editor, Cowden's family, from her grandmothers to one of her granddaughters. Many of the recipes have had the type of fat changed and/or reduced and the desserts tend to be made with fruits. Although not a diet book, the publisher and editor sought good food, easily prepared, which also tasted good. And from the trials I've made they have succeeded. As for ease of preparation, what could be easier than cookies made with only three ingredients? Not only are they easy, my husband loves them!

Included is an entire section on herbs contributed by Martha McNatt of Humboldt, Tennessee. Herb lore, recipes and a handy spice guide are presented.

While not a comprehensive cookbook, almost any Southerner who thumbs through it will be likely to say, "I remember that. My mother used to make that."

The book's small size and special optabind cover (it will lie flat and still has a spine) makes it handy to keep in the kitchen where big, heavy books usually just get in the way.

MEET THE JUDGES

Tod Marshall, Memphis, Tennessee, judged the general catagory. He is an assistant professor of English at Rhodes College; he teaches American literature and creative writing. He has taught there since receiving his Ph.D. in 1996 from the University of Kansas where his dissertation, "The Provinces of Poetry," won the Dorothy Haglund Award for the outstanding dissertation in all disciplines. He has published poetry, essays, interviews, stories, translations, and book-reviews in many journals, including *The American Poetry Review, The Iowa Review, the Southern Review*, and others. Finally he has two little boys, Lincoln and Henry; they keep him busy.

Peggy Vining, Little Rock, Arkansas, judged the humorous prose and poetry. She has directed the Arkansas Writer's Conference for the past two years. She is on the faculty of the first annual American Christian Writers Conference in Little Rock in September, 1999. Still serving on the board of the Ozark Writers Conference, she was director for 13 years. She has been nominated to receive a Governors Art Award for her involement in Arkansas Literary Arts. She is presently compiling a book of her published poetry. She has served as president, and in other leadership roles in the Poets Roundtable of Arkansas and in Arkansas National League of American Pen Women.

Rosemary Stephens, widely published author of prose, poetry, and fiction, judged the prose. Her novels were published by Scholastic Books, her stories by *Seventeen* and literary journals. She has won national awards and has appeared in university quarterlies and anthologies. Her first collection of poems, *Eve's Navel* won a publication award from South and West. She holds the Ph.D. in English from the University of Mississippi. She was first place winner of the Eve Braden Hatchett Tennessee Bicentennial Award given by *Grandmother Earth III.*

E. Marcelle Zarshenas is on the editorial staff of Grandmother Earth and is an associate of B. David Sweeney Law firm in Memphis, Tennessee. Along with Patricia Smith and Frances Cowden, she helped judge the environmental entries.

Barbara Abbott, Bartlett, Tennessee, poet and artist, is the editor of *Grandmother Earth's Healthy and Wise Cookbook.* She judged the Haiku.

Lorraine Smith, Collierville, Tennessee, judge of the short form, is a retired English and Spanish teacher and an editorial assistant for Grandmother Earth.

Patricia Smith, editor of *Grandmother Earth V,* selected the editor's choice prose.

CONTRIBUTORS' NOTES

Kareem Al-Darahi, Nashville, Tennessee, and **Leonardo Alishan**, Salt Lake City, Utah, appear for the first time in *Grandmother Earth*.

Therese Arceneaux, Lafayette, Louisianna, has been in two other issues of *Grandmother Earth*.

Patty Ashworth, Memphis, Tennessee, is author of a new collection of poetry, *Poems for a Rainy Night II*.

Dennis Beck is fromToledo, Ohio.

Burnette Bolin Benedict, Knoxville, Tennessee, is author of *Kinship*, lyrical poetry set in Tennessee a Grandmother Earth Chapbook award winner.

Helen F. Blackshear, Montgomery, Alabama, is a widely published poet and frequent contest winner. She is Poet Laureate of Alabama

Lucille Bogue's "Letter to the Editor" was winner of the 1998 Mid-South Writers Grandmother Earth Award

Najwa Salam Brax, Flushing, New York, is a bilingual poet and writer. She received her Master of Arts degree in 1983. She has won 200 awards for her poetry publishing recently in *Planeteria* (Edizioni Universum, Italy), and *Poetry Now* magazine (England). Her bio has appeared in "The 8th and 9th editions of *International Who's Who in Poetry and Poets Encyclopedia*, Cambridge-England and in *International Directory of Authors & Artists* (1997-1998) by "Creative Arts & Science Enterprises."

Barbara Brent Brower has been published in many journals and anthologies including: *The Muse Strikes Back Anthology* published by Story Line Press, *Crazy Quilt, The Lyric, Great River Review, Ruby, Tirra-Lirra* (Australia), to name a few.

Florence Bruce, Memphis, Tennessee, is a retired medical transcriptionist from Methodist Hospital and now works part-time at Baptist Hospital. She has won numerous awards and is an active member of the Lewis Center Chorus. She was graduated from Drury College in Springfield, Mo. and later earned a Master's degree in English from the University of Memphis. She is a member of the Poetry Society of Tennessee, Mid-South Writers and is associate editor of *Writers on the River*.

Maureen Cannon has been published in *Ladies Home Journal, Good Housekeeping, McCalls The Saturday Evening Post, The N.Y. Times, National Review, The Christian Science Monitor, Play-Bill, Lyric, Mature Years, Children's Digest*, etc. She teaches a light verse class locally and creative writing classes in nursing homes, schools, women's clubs and wherever she's asked. Poems have appeared in recent anthologies: *When a Lifemate Dies and the Metropolitian Diary* collection of pieces from the *N. Y. Tmes* and the The Random House, *Book of Light Verse*.

Marilyn Califf is a photographer and artist from Memphis, Tennessee.

Marcia Camp, Little Rock, Arkansas, won the Sybil Nash Abrams Award in 1984. Her poetry and prose appear in both regional and national publications.

Hollis K. Cathey lives in the Ozarks with his wife, Maurine and four dogs. "I've been writing for six years and am still learning. I attend three to four conferences yearly, including Mid-South. My office walls are adorned with many contest wins and so far this year I've sold five short stories. Also, I'm currently working on the third manuscript of a historical Western series."

Dr. Diane M. Clark is Associate Professor of Music at Rhodes College in Memphis, Tennessee. She a member of the Poetry Society of Tennessee and Associate Director of the Greater Memphis chorus of Sweet Adelines International.

Arla M. Clemons, La Crosse, Wisconsin, is a retired physical education teacher, now pursuing her writing career.

She has been published in the *Wisconsin Poets' Calendar, Touchstone, and Grandmother Earth IV.*

Cathryn Cofell of Appleton, Wisconsin, has been published often in Wisconsin, occasionally in the Midwest, and "not enough in national publications." For fun, she guest-edits other people's publications, guest-speaks at other people's classes and critiques other people's books. Her goal is to someday become that other person.

Frances Brinkley Cowden is author of *Etchings Across the Moon,* South and West (1966); *View From a Mississippi River Cotton Sack,* GEC, (1993 and 1994); and co-author of *Of Butterflies and Unicorns,* GEC (1989, 1991, 1993 and 1994); *Our Golden Thread,* Life Press(1996). She is editor of *To Love a Whale,* GEC (1995); *Tennessee Voices,* The Poetry Society of Tennessee, and the *Grandmother Earth* series. A retired English and art teacher, she is founder of Life Press Writers Association.

Margaret Cutchins is a teacher with classroom experience in Virginia and Alabama schools. She has recently retired from the Pre-School division of Lee-Scott Academy in Auburn, Alabama, whre she continues to serve as advisor to the staff of the school's literary magazine, "Smoke Signals." This is her third poem to appear in Grandmother Earth.

Reese Danley-Kilgo, Ph.D., former university professor (education and sociology) and counselor family therapist, (private practice) retired in 1988 to become a full-time writer. She likes reading and writing, gardening and grandmothering, teaching now and then, playing Scrabble with friends. She has a long list of awards and publications in poetry and fiction, has a novel and a children's book seeking a publisher.

Frances Darby, Memphis, Tennessee, is an editorial assistant for Grandmother Earth and Life Press. She is assistant director of Life Press Christian Writers' Conference. She had a poem in *Word of Mouth,* Poetry Today, Great Britain. She has articles in *Our Golden*

101

Thread, and poetry in all of the *Grandmother Earth* series. She is the widow of the late Rev. James W. Darby, a United Methodist minister.

Frieda Dorris, Memphis, Tennessee, is one of the orginators of the Dorsimbra poetry form. A past president of the Poetry Society of Tennessee, she has won numerous awards for her poetry.

Anne Marie Dyer, Kentucky Colonel, Clearwater, Florida, is a private dectective. She likes to ride horses and has a dog named Colonel. She is the niece of Cornelius Hogenbirk.

Rebecca Earle is a tenth grade student at Collierville, Tennesse.

Winifred Hamrick Farrar is Poet Laureate of Mississippi, and is widely published. She is a member of the Mississippi Poetry Society, the Poetry Society of Tennessee, and the NLAPW, Chickasaw Branch.

Evelyn Foote, Memphis, Tennessee, is a member of Mid-South Writers Association and the Poetry Society of Tennessee.

Lurlynn Franklin, Memphis, Tennesse, received a B. A. in art from Minot State University in North Dakota and an MFA from Memphis College of Art. Her paintings have been shown in local and national expositions. Also a playwright and poet she has published over 40 poems in national magazines and anthologies.

Betty Gay writes, "I'm a country girl, having lived all of my seventy-one years on a farm. My husband and I celebrated our Golden Anniversary last May in the loving company of our four children and six grandchildren. In addition to writing, my hobbies are sewing, playing classical piano music and reading." Her publications include: *Woman's World, Byline, Birdwatchers Digest, Home Life,* and *Mature Living.*

Allan Gilbreath, Memphis, Tennessee, is a computer program instructor. He appeared in *Monsters from Memphis* and *More Monsters from Memphis.* His novel, *Galen,* is a dark fantasy published by Ronin Enterprises.

Frank Govan is Professor of Art Emeritus at the University of Memphis. He has had four one man art shows in New York. His writing ability was reawakened through Writer's Forum at MIFA Senior Center.

Edith Guy is a Memphis member of the Poetry Society of Tennesse and has appeared in several Grandmother Earth publications.

J. Harding is from Pleasant Hill, California.

Ruth Peal Harrell, Memphis, Tennessee, has conducted workshops explaining Kenneth Beaudoin's eye-poems. Her publications include Voices International.

Louise Stovall Hays had a story about her great-grandfather published by the *Commercial Appeal* (Memphis, Tennessee) when she was 10. Her writing continued in her business career: fashion productions and commentaries, speeches, promotional materials. She wrote articles for *Church News*, a monthly publication for the Episcopal Diocese of West Tennessee. Currently she serves on the Vestry and is a lector for Christ Church Episcopal. She is actively involved with the Poetry Society of Tennessee, The Memphis Art League and other organizations.

Betty Lou Hebert, Coeur dAlene, Idaho, has had several environmental poems in Grandmother Earth publications, including *To Love a Whale*.

Jeanne Heath Heritage, a native Carolinian, lived in California for many years before returning to her home in Stanley, North Carolina, in 1994 to write and watch two grandchildren (10 and 14 years old) grow up. Her publications include: *The Lyric, Poet, SPSM&H, Troubadour* and *Piedmont Literary Review*. She is currently putting together a collection.

Delores Hinde, Hot Springs, Arkansas, is a member of the Poets' Roundtable of Arkansas and a frequent contest winner.

Verna Lee Hinegardner, Poet Laureate of Arkansas is a past president of the Arkansas Pioneer Branch of The National

League of American Penwomen; Past President of Poets' Roundtable of Arkansas; President of Roundtable Poets of Hot Springs; served 12 years on the board of National Federation of State Poetry Societies and chaired two of their national conventions; member of Poets' Study Club, Poetry Society of America, International Poetry Society; and is listed in The International Directory of Distinguished Leadership.

Hinegardner was inducted in the Arkansas Writers' Hall of Fame in 1991; won their Sibyl Nash Abrams Award in 1973, 1979 and 1991; received the Arkansas Award of Merit in 1976 and 1983; and is the author of nine books of poetry.

Victoria Hodge, Memphis, Tennessee. is middle school music teacher at Evangelical Christian School. Her poem, "Be Still and Know," appears on a mural she painted for Colonial Park United Methodist Church. She won a first place award with was published in *Seasons of the Soul,* Dr. R. Paul Caudill publisher.

Ann and Jerry Hoffman, Ft. Smith, Arkansas, are members of the Poets' Roundtable of Arkansas, Oklahoma Writer's Federation Incorporated, Arkansas Ridgewriters, and the Poetry Society of Tennessee. They are frequent contest winners. Jerry won the Sybil Nash Abrams Award in 1996. He is a retired Air Force veteran with a Masters in Education from the University of the Ozarks. Ann is an LPN and takes care of special needs adults.

Cornelius Hogenbirk, of Waretown, New Jersey is a retired sales engineer. His hobbies are photography, gardening and writing. His work has been in every issue of *Grandmother Earth*, sometimes under the name of Neal Hogenbirk.

Elizabeth Howard, Crossville, Tennessee, is the author of *Anemones,* Grandmother Earth, 1998 which contains poetry that has been previously published in journals and anthologies. She is a frequent award-winner.

Lois Batchelor Howard says, "Music is my vocation, and, between teaching and practicing and performing, the available time to write is brief, often just long enough for a poem to be written or begun. In 1996, I had a poem and a photograph published in *Grandmother Earth.*"

Jennifer A. Jenson is an attorney in Memphis, Tennessee.

Charles H. Johnson's poetry has appeared in various literary magazines, newspapers and online, and soon will be published in "Lips," "Connecticut Review" and "Footwork: The Patterson Literary Review." He has won several awards for his work, including a first place in the 1998 Allen Ginsberg Poetry Awards. He is poetry reviewer and copy desk chief for the *Home News Tribune* in East Brunswick, New Jersey.

Judith Bader Jones is doing a line of cards using her photographs of flowers. Though from Fairway, Kansas, she has ties to Tennessee which include a grandmother named Tennessee.

Nellie Jones, Walls, Mississippi,has been an active member of the Poetry Society of Tennessee for several years. She is a retired social worker and is a feature writer for *Women's News of the Mid-South.*

Michael Kass, Memphis, Tennessee, was given a President's Scholar Award at Stanford University, Palo Alto, California, where he is now a sophomore. His creative writing portfolio included publication in Grandmother Earth when he was a student at White Station High School. He is using his scholarship for creative writing.

Carley Kiel is a 15-year old student at White Station High School, Memphis, Tennessee. She has won several awards with her poetry.

Floyd Knight, Jamestown, California, is a retired accountant and author of a poetry book, *Eye of the Beholder.* Part-time columnist for the Modesto (CA) Bee, is a World War II veteran. An active Octogenarian, he enjoys golf, billiards, hiking, table tennis, poker, etc. His late wife, Martha, was a prolific writer, columnist and musician.

Michael Lucas, St. Louis, Missouri, has a BFA from Memphis Academy of Art. He is an exhibitor at the St. Louis Museum of Art.

Martha McNatt, Humboldt, Tennessee, is a former teacher, and director of the Child Nutrition Program for Madison County Schools. She is the author of *Feeding the Flock,* a cookbook for church kitchens, published by Bethany House, and *A Heritage Revisited,* a commissioned work by First Christian Church, Jackson, Tennessee. Her work has appeared in each of the Grandmother Earth anthologies, in *Grandmother Earth's Healthy and Wise Cookbook,* and in Life Press's *Our Golden Thread.* Martha is president of the Jackson Circle Branch of the National League of American Pen Women.

Margot Marler, Rossville, Georgia has had work in every issue of *Grandmother Earth.* She has sent copies of each issue to several libraries in her area.

Jane Mayfield, Milan, Tennessee, owns a beauty salon and art studio combination, "Reflections, Hair and Art." A frequent award winner, this is her first published drawing. She is chairperson of the annual UT West Tennessee Agricultural Museum exhibition.

Houstonian **Dodie Messer Meeks,** has appeared in The Anthology of Magazine Verse and Yearbook of American Poetry; Visions International, the Unitarian-Universalist Anthology and The Southwest Review, and celebrates dotage with a series entitled: "Things That Scare The Kids." She said she would love to hear from other water colorists and or poets through her web-page: Dodiemeeks@juno.com http://web.wt.net/~dodie

Marjorie Millison, La Conner, Washington, writes, "We are retired and spend much of our time enjoying the beauty of the N.W. with our trailer. It enables us to visit the ocean, mountains, rivers, lakes, and forests. We are especially awed by the old-growth forests. We also have spent years exploring the islands of the N.W in our boat. We feel we are truly blessed.

Tammy D. Moon, Smithville, Tennessee, is a member of Cookeville Writers Association.

Eleanor Moore, Cordova, Tennessee, is a new-comer to Grandmother Earth.

Anne Norris, Memphis, Tennessee is a member of the Memphis Story Tellers' League.

June Owens, Zephyrhills, Florida, is a frequent national award winner.

Debra Parmley has been published in Bellowing *Ark, Poetalk, and Poetic Realm.* She recently moved to Tennessee from the Pocono Mountains in Pennsylvania and currently works at the Collierville Herald in advertising.

Tracy Patterson, Memphis, Tennessee and **Timothy Russell**, Toronto, Ohio, are new-comers to Grandmother Earth.

Barbara A. Rouillard, Springfield, Massachusetts, has poetry or short stories which have appeared in publication, or is forthcoming in *Amelia, Midwest Poetry Review, Palo Alto Review, Slur, Happy, The Northern Centinel, The Valley Optimist, Feminist Voices, Art and Understanding, Writer's Journal, David's Place, Byline, 96 Inc., Poetry in Motion,* and *Verve.* In 1994 she recieved a National Endowment for the Humanities Fellowship for an independent study of twentieth century American female poets.

Florence Holmes Ryan, Memphis, Tennessee, is a member of the Poetry Society of Tennesse and the Memphis Branch of NLAPW. She has been published frequently in *Voices International, Tennessee Voices* and *Old Hickory Review.*

LaVonne Schoneman is from Seattle, Washington.

Robert (Bob) **S. Shelford** is president of First Florida Poets at DeLand, Florida, and an adjunct instructor of formal poetry writing at Daytona Beach Community College. He is an active member of the Florida State Poet's Assn. and in January will become editor of the FSPA quarterly publication--OF POETS AND POETRY. A native of New Jersey, he spent his working years as a writer/editor in Albany, NY. He retired in 1984 and moved to DeLand.

D. Beecher Smith, II is a widely published poet, writer and editor as well as a prominent Memphis, Tennessee, attorney. He is editor-in-chief and publisher of Hot Biscuits Productions. "Faith Vs. the Dark Angel," appeared originally in *Angel Whispers* and is reprinted in *Angels: Messengers of Love and Grace*. He is editor of *Monsters from Memphis* and *More Monsters from Memphis*.

Patricia W. Smith, Memphis, Tennessee, is editor of the *Grandmother Earth* Series. The poem which appeared in this collection is reprinted from *Grandmother Earth IV*. Very active in the Poetry Society of Tennessee, she is currently its president. She is also state president of the National League of American Pen Woman for Tennessee.

Russell H. Strauss, Memphis, Tennessee, is an officer of the Poetry Society of Tennessee, and wins numerous awards. The poems included here were first-place winners and are reprinted from a *Tennessee Voices* anthology (PST, Memphis).

Larry Sutton, Terry, Tennessee, cousin of Jane Mayfield, started writing poetry after the recent loss of his wife. This is his first time to be published.

Dr. Marla Treece is Professor Emeritus, College of Business and Economics, University of Memphis. She is author of thirteen college textbooks and has just published the seventh edition of *Successful Communication for Business and the Profession.*

Ida Crane Walker, Hot Springs, Arkansas, is a national contest winner and a member of Poets Roundtable and the Pioneer Branch of the NLAPW.

Florine Petkoff Walters, Helena, Arkansas, has been a member of Poets' Roundtable of Arkansas since 1970, a member of East Central Branch of Poets Roundtable for as long and an associate member of Poetry Society of Tennessee since 1979.

Timothy D. Welch, Corona Del Mar, California, appears for the first time in Grandmother Earth.

Jackie Marie White -- Blytheville, Arkansas, is one of the organizers of the Mississippi County Writers Contest. She wins many regional and national awards.

Opal Harper Wooldridge is a free lance writer who currently resides in Springfield, Tennessee. A former resident of Blytheville, Arkansas, she continues to be a member of the Mississippi County Writers Guild (Blytheville) and the Poets Round Table of Arkansas. She has served on the board of the American Gourd Society and has enjoyed sharing her knowledge of gourds with various groups.

Kitty Yeager, Arkadelphia, Arkansas, is a life member of the Poets' Round Table of Arkansas and the Poetry Society of Tennessee. She wins national awards frequently.

CONTRIBUTING PATRONS

C&J Trophy and Engraving Service
3444 Park Avenue, Memphis, TN 38111
452-5393 or 452-0100

Dr. John D. McVean
Dentist
124 Timber Creek
Cordova, Tennessee, 38018

Clay's Audio
2544 Summer Avenue
Memphis, Tennessee 38112
452-4022

Mr. Z Imports
Sound Equipment
245 N. Cleveland
Memphis, Tennessee 38104

T Π T Pro-Audio
1720 Winchester
Memphis, Tennessee 38116
901-332-4277

Dee Kass in honor of
Michael Kass and Carly Kiel

IN HONOR OF HAZEL DARBY VAUGHAN

Our Shining Light for 93 Years
Frances Darby

ANTIQUES *plus*

MALL AND AUCTION
MARION, ARKANSAS
EXIT 14 -- I -55
5 MILES NORTH OF WEST MEMPHIS

Antiques of all types.
"We buy estate merchandise."
Call 501-739-5856

IN CELEBRATION: MY BELOVED GUSTAVE
Benevolent Humanitarian
In God's hands
In my heart

Rita Lurie

IN MEMORY OF DR. D. SHELBY COUNCE
June 22, 1923--May 19, 1998
Husband of Christine Counce

IN MEMORY OF CHESTER GARFIELD RIDER
June 15, 1915--December 19, 1997
Husband of Dr. Wanda Rider

IN MEMORY OF EVA M. STEEN
December 30, 1913--March 30, 1998
Mother of Betty Smith
Grandmother of Brian Smith

ANGELS: MESSENGERS OF LOVE AND GRACE

Frances Brinkley Cowden
Editor
Martha McNatt
Contributing Editor

ISBN 1-884289-18-5 9.95, 96 pages, perfect bound.

Was it an angel? Could it have been anything else? All of these stories have one thing in common, the belief that the angel or angels brought a message of God's love to each individual's life. Frances Brinkley Cowden, founder of Life Press, brings experiences of people from all walks of life varying from the certainty of seeing, touching or hearing an angel to raising questions.

Why do angels intervene in some instances and not in others? Our purpose is not to explain God's mysteries but to glorify Him. This book expects to raise more questions than it answers. It is with humility and gratitude that the twenty-three contributors share their stories.

LIFE PRESS WRITERS ASSOCIATION
P. O. Box 241986
Memphis, Tennessee 38124

Help for beginning or seldom-published writers. Emphasis is upon writing for Christian publications, but we will critique all types of writing.

Quarterly newsletter with lessons and assignments. Individual critiques 3 poems or pages of prose per quarter. $15 per year.

***

GRANDMOTHER EARTH PUBLICATIONS

Abbott, Barbara, GRANDMOTHER *EARTH'S HEALTHY AND WISE COOKBOOK*, 1-884289-13-4 Healthy and easy cooking, but not diet. First layer of fat skimmed from Southern cooking. Optabind binding; $14.

Benedict, Burnette Bolin, *KINSHIP*, 1-884289-08-8 Lyrical poetry set in eastern Tennessee by Knoxville poet. Chapbook, 1995, $6.

Cowden, Frances Brinkley, *VIEW FROM A MISSISSIPPI RIVER COTTON SACK*--1-884289-03-7, Poetry, family values of farm life in Mississippi County, Arkansas. Cloth, gold imprint, 1993, $15.

TO LOVE A WHALE; 1-884289-O6-1. Learning about endangered animals from children and adults. Children's drawings, poetry and prose, Perfect bound, 1995, $10.00

BUTTERFLIES AND UNICORNS, ED 4, 1-884289-04-5 (Cowden and Hatchett) Poetry for the young and young-at-heart with notes on teaching creative writing. Perfect bound, 1994, $8.00

115

Daniel, Jack, *SOUTHERN RAILWAY: FROM STEVENSON TO MEMPHIS*--1-884289-17-7 1/2x11 with 400+ photographs, 360 pages, perfect bound, 1996. Signed and numbered upon request. Documents and other papers with heavy emphasis upon history of Southern Railway and its workers, $24. *MY RECOLLECTIONS OF CHEROKEE, ALABAMA*, 1-884289-25-8, 1/2x11. 300+ photographs of author's family history and life in early Cherokee, 232 pages, perfect bound, 1998, $20.

Hatchett, Eve Braden, TAKE *TIME TO LAUGH: It's the Music of the Soul.* 1- 884289-00-2, Humorous poetry taking off on Eden theme. Chapbook, limited edition, 1993, $9.

Howard, Elizabeth, *ANEMONES*, 1-884289-27-4, Prize-winning poetry, all previously published, West Tennessee poet, introduction by Connie Green. 1998, $8.95

Schirz, Shirley Rounds, *ASHES TO OAK*, 1-884289-07-X Poetry of the lakes region by widely-published Wisconsin author, chapbook winner, 1995, $6.

SUBSCRIPTION OR DIRECT ORDERS ONLY: $8 per year (otherwise $10 each)

1-884289-09-6, *GRANDMOTHER EARTH I:* 1995
1-884289-14-2, *GRANDMOTHER EARTH II:* 1996
1-884289-16-9, *GRANDMOTHER EARTH III:* 1997
1-884289-21-5, *GRANDMOTHER EARTH IV:* 1998
1-884289-24-X *GRANDMOTHER EARTH V: 1999*

LIFE PRESS PUBLICATIONS

Boren, Blanche S., *THORNS TO VELVET: Devotionals from a Lifetime of Christian Experience.* 1-884289-231, Blanche S. Boren, Kivar 7 cloth, 174 pages with 14 photographs. Uplifting look at life's experiences. 1998, $20.

Cowden, Frances Brinkley, *OUR GOLDEN THREAD: Dealing with Grief,* 1-884289-10-x, Ed. Contains personal testimonies and poetry of 40 contributors who deal with different kinds of grief using their personal faith. Kivar 7 cloth, gold imprint, 1996, $15.
ANGELS: MESSENGERS OF LOVE AND GRACE, 1-884289-18-5, True stories of angel experiences, 96 pages, perfect bound, 1999, $9.95

Crow, Geraldine Ketchum, *BLOOM WHERE YOU ARE TRANSPLANTED*: Humorous and inspirational approach to moving from the city to the country. 1-884289-12-6 paper, 1996, $10.

Davis, Elaine Nunnally, *MOTHERS OF JESUS: FROM MATTHEW'S GENEALOGY,* 1-884289-05-3-- Biblical biography of the five women mentioned in Matthew. 344 pp. Perfect binding, 1994, $12.
EVE'S FRUIT, 1-884289-11-8--Defense of Eve and implications for the modern woman. Perfect binding, 1995, $10.

Special prices may not apply unless ordered from the publisher. Add $1. 50 postage for one book plus $.50 each additional book. Mail order to Grandmother Earth and Life Press, P. O. Box 241986, Memphis, TN 38124.

INDEX